Pop Pickers Music AND Vendors

Pop Pickers and Music Vendors

David Jacobs, Alan Freeman, John Peel, Tommy Vance and Roger Scott

JOHN VAN DER KISTE

FONTHILL

I was lucky enough to grow up in an era when radio was less formatted. It was really special. You could hear a jazz song, then a pop song, then a show tune, then some jazz. Basically, whatever the DJ felt like playing, he would play. He was educating you and exposing you to things you would never hear otherwise.

Todd Rundgren, 2014

Fonthill Media Language Policy

Fonthill Media publishes in the international English language market. One language edition is published worldwide. As there are minor differences in spelling and presentation, especially with regard to American English and British English, a policy is necessary to define which form of English to use. The Fonthill Policy is to use the form of English native to the author. John Van der Kiste was born and educated in England; therefore British English has been adopted in this publication.

Fonthill Media Limited
Fonthill Media LLC
www.fonthillmedia.com
office@fonthillmedia.com

First published in the United Kingdom and the United States of America 2016

British Library Cataloguing in Publication Data:
A catalogue record for this book is available from the British Library

Copyright © John Van der Kiste 2016

ISBN 978-1-78155-544-6

The right of John Van der Kiste to be identified as the author of this work has been asserted by him in accordance with the Copyright, Designs and Patents Act 1988.

All rights reserved. No part of this publication may be reproduced, stored in a retrieval system or transmitted in any form or by any means, electronic, mechanical, photocopying, recording or otherwise, without prior permission in writing from Fonthill Media Limited

Typeset in 10.5pt on 13pt Sabon
Printed and bound in England

Foreword

Most biographies of that unloved breed 'disc jockeys' are littered with blunders and errors because their author arrives at the character from too subjective a viewpoint. Maybe they're writing to a budget, regurgitating the opinions of someone they met in a pub once, or simply too bloody lazy to check anything beyond the name of the character—and trust me, they get that wrong sometimes.

Of course, it is true that they're often not helped by cuttings and quotes.

In the fine tradition of footpads, cut-throats, and circus performers, and in an attempt to make themselves interesting, most DJs have reinvented themselves as often as needed, quoting fiction and self-interest in equal parts, perfectly reasonably, in self-interest and fear of unemployment—but above all terrified of being thought dull.

Here, though, it's different.

John Van der Kiste is the first to sift through the mountain of fiction and present his subjects calmly, affectionately, with a few warts attached, and in context, and bless him for it. What you'll get here is a fond and accurate look at five of the most familiar voices of the last fifty years—and, along the way, a glimpse of the shades that lurk behind all broadcasters.

The bullshit and the politics.

The management.

Simon Bates

Acknowledgments

This book would certainly not have been possible without the help of a few individuals who have been generous with their time in their reminiscences about working with the DJ, or supplying cuttings, downloads of radio documentaries, and other data.

I am especially grateful to Tim Blackmore, Claire Sturgess, Phil Swern, and Sue and Mike Woolmans, with whom I have had very enlightening conversations on the phone. In the process, they provided me with much first-hand information about all five presenters, and in some cases also supplied downloads of archive sound material. Andy Walmsley's Random Radio Jottings website has proved invaluable, as have the various items of information and images he has sent me in the course of my research. Marc Denis has contributed some priceless memories and photographs of Roger Scott in Montreal and London. Mary and Chris Payne from the Radio London website have helped with photographs, sending several invaluable links and contacting others on my behalf. Lesley-Ann Jones, writer, broadcaster and author, 'Softly' (Jon Adrian), and Nicky Horne have all provided recollections, as has Jon Myer, who read through the draft and pointed out a few inaccuracies. Jamie Scott was very generous in providing me with images of his father, Roger. Derek Tait pointed me in the direction of some useful material online, and the Radio Rewind website has also proved a marvellous internet resource for its background detail on various presenters and its magnificent collection of audio clips. Details of these sites and others can be found in the bibliography. Several people who contributed material read through all or part of the manuscript, helpfully indicating errors and making useful suggestions, while Nikki Geary proved, as ever, an excellent proofreader.

Last but not least, I would like to thank Simon Bates for his foreword, my wife, Kim, for her unfailing support throughout, particularly with regard to being among those who read the manuscript on completion and assisted with general ideas for improvement. I would also like to thank my editors at Fonthill Media, Jay Slater and Joe Tranter, for their help in seeing the work through to publication.

John Van der Kiste

Contents

Foreword   5
Acknowledgements   6
Introduction   9

1 David Jacobs   13

2 Alan Freeman   33

3 John Peel   60

4 Tommy Vance   90

5 Roger Scott   110

Endnotes   129
Bibliography   135
Index   137

Introduction

Since the advent of sound broadcasting, disc jockeys have often had a less than favourable image in the press. In the early 1970s, the broadcaster and would-be Liberal MP Ludovic Kennedy pontificated that DJs had 'no vocabulary apart from grunts'.[1] Disc jockeys were fair game in those days. Comedian Jasper Carrott later said that he was 'amazed at radio DJs today'. He added, 'I am firmly convinced that AM on my radio stands for "Absolute Moron". I will not begin to tell you what "FM" stands for.'[2] It is safe to assume that the latter's remarks were meant to be taken rather less seriously than those of the former.

Nevertheless, as with those in other walks of the entertainment sphere, there are quality presenters and those who are less so. Radio disc jockeys have generally been divisible into those who are or were motivated by a love of the music they play, and those who saw it as just another branch of showbusiness, if not a stepping stone to something else. In the 1950s, some of them came into broadcasting almost by accident, or for want of an alternative. They ended up discovering a quasi-evangelical zeal to share the music they presented with their most devoted listeners, some of whom would write in to ask which record they played on their show on such-and-such a day. In time, they often went on to inspire a new generation.

In this book, I have taken five of the disc jockeys whom I regard as among the greatest in their field, and whose careers spanned six decades of musical change, from the 1950s to the 2010s. Perhaps it is significant that not only did each of them end their careers as radio presenters, but also that four of them were still broadcasting within weeks of their passing away; the fifth was only forced into retirement after more than forty years when ill-health made it physically impossible for him to continue. This book is intended to be an affectionate and hopefully informed look at those who, at various times, towered above the commanding heights in their chosen vocation. I could easily name a few more from the ranks of those still living and on air at the present time, but in the present context I felt it was better to devote attention to five of the seminal names no longer with us.

My original working title for the book was *Eminent DJs*, inspired largely by Lytton Strachey's *Eminent Victorians*. I am glad to note that others evidently regard at least two of them as eminent (illustrious, distinguished, renowned, so an online dictionary tells me), and that Alan Freeman and John Peel have taken their rightful places in the *Oxford Dictionary of National Biography*. Sir Ludovic Kennedy, as he was by the time of his death, is in distinguished company, whether he likes it or not.

Many of us grew up listening to pop music on the radio; some even refused to grow out of the habit as we grew older and wiser, despite having a previous generation probably telling us (with a degree of firmness) that we ought to know better. We must have heard many presenters in our time. Some may have been so-so, others even irritating, but the best of them added a certain *je ne sais quoi* in between the records they played. As Derek Chinnery, Controller of Radio 1, sarcastically told the independently-minded and soon-to-be-fired Johnnie Walker in the summer of 1976, the trouble with him was that he was 'too into the music'.[3] It is a description, maybe even a compliment, that surely applies to the five under scrutiny here. To an extent, they eschewed the cult of personality in their presentation of the music they loved and were so keen to share with their listeners.

One of the subjects, if not all five of them, certainly believed as much. When he was originally committing ideas to paper for what would eventually become his published memoirs (completed mainly by his widow, Sheila, after his sudden death), John Peel noted: 'Musings on the great DJs (a contradiction in terms?) … and the only British-based Great DJ, Alan Freeman'.[4]

In the course of my research, I have made use of much material from various print sources and online, as indicated by the bibliography. As is so often the case, some sources have proved more than a little contradictory. If you believe all you read, Tommy Vance was born in 1940, 1941, and 1943, though a straw poll suggests that the first of these dates is the more popular choice. It also goes without saying that there is probably more material on John Peel than on the other four put together. Two biographies were published within months of his death, while his memoir, a volume of his collected writings, and two more volumes have followed since. Neither David Jacobs, Alan Freeman, Tommy Vance, nor Roger Scott have received anything like the same attention, and only the first of them ever published an autobiography—quite early in his career, too. Moreover, as one of the most authoritative of Peel experts, Ken Garner, has stated, many of his obituaries were strewn with howlers.[5] I would respectfully like to think that my researches have saved me from falling into the same trap too often.

I have done my best to cite references for quotations and sources. Those which remain uncited are either from my own (hopefully mostly accurate) memory, acquired over several decades of listening to and watching my five subjects on radio and television, personal information contributed by those mentioned in the Acknowledgements, and material online for which either no precise source is given, or which has been duplicated word-for-word in a number of places.

1
David Jacobs

In the late 1950s and early 1960s, pop music in Britain was good, clean, light entertainment for the whole family. Rock 'n roll had lost its cutting edge and was no longer looked on as the downfall of Western civilisation that some commentators feared it might be when they first listened to and saw pictures and footage of Bill Haley and his Comets, Elvis Presley, Chuck Berry and Little Richard with varying degrees of dread. Conductor Sir Malcolm Sargent had dismissed it as something that had 'been played in the jungle for centuries' and 'nothing more than an exhibition of primitive tom-tom thumping', while songwriter Billy Rose called Elvis Presley's repertoire 'obscene junk, pretty much on a level with dirty comic magazines'.[1] Once the shock of the new had ceased to horrify, critics and listeners accepted it even if they did not embrace it wholeheartedly. There was absolutely nothing threatening about any of the clean-cut British stars such as Cliff Richard and the Shadows, Adam Faith and the Roulettes or Frank Ifield. Even The Beatles—once they had been smartened up, lectured about general deportment and professionalism by their savvy manager Brian Epstein, and moulded into an accomplished musical unit by classical-musician-turned-producer George Martin—were not the menace that they might have longed to be in their more iconoclastic moods. As for The Rolling Stones, despite their unwashed, scruffy appearance, at heart they were by and large nice lads who really wanted fame and fortune and were prepared to play the showbusiness game up to a point.

Over this music scene towered one formidable radio and television presenter—the affable, gentlemanly David Jacobs. He would be an ever-reliable, almost-unchanging stalwart of British broadcasting for over half a century.

David Lewis Jacobs was born in Streatham Hill, London, on 19 May 1926, the youngest of three sons. His father, also called David, was a Covent Garden fruit importer who went bankrupt in 1939 after a period of ill-health and the failure of his business. Young David left school at the age of fourteen and took various short-term jobs. He was successively a stable boy, a farm hand, an errand boy, a pawnbroker's clerk, and an assistant to a gent's outfitter, before joining the Royal Navy at the age of eighteen. This led to brief appearances on the BBC General Forces Programme *Navy Mixture*, doing impressions, before he realised that stand-up comedy was not going to be his greatest strength. A naval officer heard one of his broadcasts and told him he did not think much of his impersonations, 'but he thought the way I announced them was very good'.[2] It resulted in his becoming an announcer with the British Forces Broadcasting Service and on Radio SEAC (South East Asian Command) in Ceylon from 1945 to 1947. Radio SEAC was the wartime radio station operated by the Allied Forces who took over the operations of Colombo Radio, the Ceylonese radio station launched in 1925, and David later became assistant station director for a while.

By the end of the decade, David had his foot firmly in the door at the BBC. On being told that the Corporation's overseas service was desperately short of announcers and that his name had been put forward, he was interviewed and taken on. He survived an initial *faux pas* by asking how long it would be before he graduated to the Home or Light Programmes, a question that was greeted by stony silence.

It was not the only mishap of his younger days. One evening, while reading the home news, he managed to get through an amusing item about a delivery of eggs from Poland while keeping a straight face. At that point a sub-editor walked over to him, brandishing a sheet of paper featuring what was presumably an urgent piece of news just in. He glanced at it to see a photograph of, in his own words, 'a remarkably unclad young woman', and could not help bursting into laughter. Somehow he managed to take a deep breath and say that it was the end of the news—five minutes too soon. The next day he was summoned to the Head of Presentation's office and told that his services would no longer be required.[3] Fortunately, the guilty party owned up to having been responsible and David was reinstated. However, a tendency to laugh at inappropriate times on air remained one of his failings. When he found a new role as Benny Hill's straight man on the latter's radio show, he found it impossible to contain his mirth most of the time and lasted just one programme before being fired.

His career as a young staff announcer would be the stepping stone to greater things. In January 1949, he was chosen to introduce the pioneering radio request show *Housewives' Choice*. Determined to leave nothing to chance, at the end of his first week he wrote himself several letters telling himself how good he was, signing them with various male and female aliases. Unfortunately the BBC, 'scrupulously refraining from poking its nose into other people's business,' duly forwarded them all to him—unopened.[4] His voice would also be heard on many of the fifty-three episodes of a space adventure series, *Journey into Space*, in which he played twenty-two parts.

Although always thought of as a BBC man through and through, David also did voiceovers for adverts and recorded shows for Radio Luxembourg, which was for years the only commercial radio station in competition with the Corporation. While a few broadcasts were made live from the grand duchy studio itself, around 80 per cent of its output was pre-recorded in its London office studios. These thirty-minute shows, most of which were sponsored by Bournvita or EMI Records and continued until 1968, included *Woodbine Quiz Time*, *Pops Past Midnight*, *David Jacobs' Startime*, and *David Jacobs Plays the Pops*. They were produced by Ken Evans, who would work with David again on Radio 2 many years later.

At first he thought of calling himself David Lincoln, but then decided against it as the initials 'DJ' were more appropriate.

> I have never thought of myself as a disc-jockey as it seems to me a marginally derogatory term, perhaps because it is American. A lot of people found American cars unattractive and I am a bit that way about the American disc-jockeys.[5]

As an up-and-coming personality in the media, David had regular opportunities to meet some of those whom he had long worshipped from afar, a number of whom—ironically—were American themselves. One of his favourite encounters, one he treasured to the end of his days, was during a Variety Club dinner in the 1950s, where he sat between Judy Garland and the former Prime Minister Earl Attlee. As he rose to his feet and welcomed the Hollywood superstar to the assembled company, he turned to her with a smile and said, 'I've been in love with you for many years, though I have to admit I haven't always been faithful.' He then sat down to a huge laugh, after which Attlee leaned across and whispered in his ear, 'Who is Judy Garland?'[6] For once, David was lost for words.

Another occasion was one of a series of interviews he hosted on Radio Luxembourg with artists like Ruby Murray, Alma Cogan, and Frank Sinatra. The latter's career was going through something of a lull at the time; he was happy to appear, but on the condition that no reference should be made to his second wife, from whom he was in the process of being divorced. As he walked into the studio, his first words were, 'If you mention Ava [Gardner], I'll push the microphone down your throat.'[7] David took the hint. Later, when he was a guest of the Sinatras at home, they had a discussion about his favourite artists. Frank happily reeled off the names of Ella Fitzgerald, Tony Bennett, and Vic Damone, but as for British singers, he said that one stood out—Matt Monro.

David also had the honour of introducing Frank at a gala performance in London attended by Queen Elizabeth II. Just before they went on stage, he was sitting down, waiting for the call, while Frank was walking around. David offered him a seat, but he refused, saying, 'I know my voice is in good order, but when I go out on stage, I don't want to be in a creased suit like you.'[8]

In the mid-1950s there was a sea-change in popular music. The hit parade, as the chart was known at first, had been dominated mostly by performers such as Vera Lynn, Bing Crosby, and Rosemary Clooney. Al Martino had topped the first British chart, which was published in November 1952. Less than two years later, Bill Haley and his Comets recorded 'Rock Around The Clock', and David was the first broadcaster to play it on British radio. When it topped the American and then the British charts early in 1955, it was to be a sign that nothing would ever be the same again. In October of that year, the BBC Light Programme introduced a new show, *Pick of the Pops*, introduced firstly by Franklin Engelmann and then by Alan Dell. David took over in March 1958, presenting it late on Saturday night for the next three and a half years.

The BBC record programmes were severely restricted by a Musicians' Union 'needle time' agreement that placed major restrictions on the number of records that could be broadcast each day; this was in order to accommodate live music from orchestras, dance bands, and, later, guest vocalists providing their own versions of contemporary hits. It might have provided adequate employment and remuneration for union members, but it was not always what listeners wanted. At a time when BBC needle time was severely restricted, *Pick of the Pops* was one of the few national pop radio shows at the time, and it was the first to include the Top 20.

By now David was several years into a career that had seen him appearing as a radio and TV presenter in addition to several acting roles, both comic and straight. The latter included his first-ever television appearance in *The Amazing Adventures of Commander Highprice* in 1947, starring Jon Pertwee. Three years later, David appeared in a dramatisation of *Little Women*, and around the same time he appeared in *Puffney Post Office*, a radio comedy series starring Pertwee and Eric Barker. On the Light Programme and Home Service, he was one of several presenters of *Jazz Club,* and he provided the announcements for *She Shall Have Music,* a show in 1954 featuring trumpet player Gracie Cole and her All-Girl Orchestra. Among his other shows in the 1950s were *Purely for Pleasure, On the Brighter Side* (which was his first with producer and future Radio 1 Controller Derek Chinnery), and *Grande Gingold* (starring Hermione Gingold). He also appeared in *Saturday Show,* which featured Cyril Stapleton and the BBC Show Band and Alfred Marks; it was produced by Johnnie Stewart, the man who was later largely responsible for the creation of *Top of the Pops*. Finally, David appeared in *The Man About Town* (a star vehicle for Jack Buchanan, also featuring Vanessa Lee and Pat Coombs) and *Curiouser and Curiouser* (on which he and Peter Sellers read a selection of comic verse).

On television, once he had decided that his abilities lay in presenting and chairing as opposed to acting, he assumed voiceover duties for *Movietone News* in 1955, taking over from announcer Leslie Mitchell, who had just joined the new ITV service and recommended him as a replacement. He was also the anchorman on *Dateline London*, a series of programmes for the North American Service of the BBC in which he interviewed major American stars who were visiting Britain. He was also the anchorman for *Top Town Tournament*, in which various British towns took part in a talent contest looking for the best variety acts, a precursor to shows like *Opportunity Knocks* and *Britain's Got Talent*. One show that David preferred not to recall too often was a one-off BBC venture in 1955—*Music, Music, Music*. It featured a panel of guests who had to identify songs and tunes that were tapped out with a pencil, played backwards, sped up, or disguised in other ways. His verdict was that 'it might have kept a couple of schoolboys amused for part of a wet afternoon'. From 1959 to 1962, he also fronted *The Wednesday Magazine*, a daytime show aimed at housewives.

As he was not under exclusive contract to the BBC, David was inevitably headhunted by the new commercial ITV. In its first year, he presented the short-lived series *Focus on Hocus*, featuring magic tricks by David Berglas. The following year, he was the announcer on *The Vera Lynn Show*. Two game and panel shows followed between 1956 and 1958; the first was *Make Up Your Mind!*, on which sharp-eyed competitors could demonstrate their skill or powers of guesswork by identifying which was worth more, a specific object or a certain sum of money, with prizes for viewers and for studio challengers. It was followed by the more successful *Tell the Truth*, which had a regular panel of John Skeaping, Jacqueline Curtis, Roberta Leigh, and Bill Owen.

However, David only truly became a household name as the presenter of one the pioneering music shows on BBC television between 1959 and 1967. In 1958, the BBC decided it would launch its own version of a popular American show, *Jukebox Jury*, in which a panel would listen to and comment on a selection of new record releases and try to forecast whether they would be hits or misses. It was originally to be called *Hit or Miss*, with Jacobs, now one of the BBC's star presenters, as a member of the panel due to his track record as a disc jockey. He suggested that he had far more experience as a chairman than as a panellist, and that the American title (with a minor variation, possibly for legal reasons) should be preferred. Each week, in front of a studio audience, a panel of four jurors (mostly taken from the entertainment world) would listen to around ninety seconds from six or seven new singles and vote on them. A 'hit' would be the signal for Jacobs to hit a bell on his desk, and a 'miss' for a hooter. If the panel was equally split on a record's chances, a back-up jury of three from the studio audience would provide a joint casting vote.

One of the most regular panellists was Pete Murray, a fellow BBC broadcaster with whom David enjoyed a friendly rivalry. Pete had a regular radio show on the Light Programme on Sunday evening, the day after David's went out, and naturally they were urged to put in a gentle plug for each other. Both of them thought it would be rather boring for their listeners if they just kept to a straightforward 'don't forget to listen to so-and-so'. In order to liven things up, they decided to indulge in a little game of mock insults along the lines of 'if you've got nothing better to do I suppose you might like to listen to David Jacobs on Saturday night—but God help you if you do', and *vice versa*.

The banter entered their television appearances to an extent that sometimes startled and even offended audiences at home, unaware that it was all in jest. On the first programme, after he was introduced, Pete looked straight-facedly at the camera and assured viewers that he had nothing against David Jacobs. 'I think the world needs men like him,' he said. 'In fact, there's a very good job going for him in the gentlemen's lavatory in Leicester Square Underground Station.'

'Thanks,' quipped David, 'mention my name and you'll get a good seat.'[9] Such an exchange would hardly raise an eyebrow today, but for the TV audience of the late 1950s, this was beyond the pale. It certainly went against the rules of a BBC variety programmes' 1948 policy guide for writers and producers, which expressly forbade any references to 'lavatories, effeminacy in men, [or] immorality of other kind', and various other subjects, such as religion, which risked causing offence in those straitened times. Several viewers immediately phoned the switchboard to complain. Eric Maschwitz, Head of Light Entertainment at BBC Television, was furious, and both culprits received a severe dressing-down. They presumably did not promise not to do it again, but a more liberal regime at the Corporation would soon prevail, ushered in by the anarchic *That Was The Week That Was* in 1963 and other shows of a similar nature.

Most of the guests were unfailingly charming, but a few were not beyond causing their chairman the odd problem. Zsa Zsa Gabor agreed to appear on the panel one week. However, she insisted that David and all the male guests had to wear black ties and dinner jackets on the show because she simply had to wear her diamonds, and she could not possibly do so unless they were in evening dress as well. She also told David that he had to take her out for lunch before the recording; his explanation that he had already promised to take his children out for the day cut no ice with her. After a fulsome apology to the family, lunch with her at the Caprice and an anxious discussion with his producer, Johnnie Stewart, he managed to make her change her mind on the matter of attire by informing her that the royal family never dressed for dinner before 6.45 p.m., and the programme went out from 6.00 to 6.30.[10]

Artists, David observed, were generally professionals; they might be awkward, even temperamental, but they always knew that the show must go on. As in the case of another star invited as a panellist one week, they might even be a little frightening. Eartha Kitt, he found, had 'a disturbing presence and disturbing habits', and sometimes stared at him while she said nothing at all, which was even more disconcerting. Then she would defuse the situation by admitting that she was not really wicked, fixing him with her very bright eyes and then delivering 'an almighty pinch in the biceps'.[11]

Most panellists were much older than the artists whose records they were reviewing. There was something a little odd about choosing the likes of Spike Milligan, Nancy Spain, Thora Hird, Eric Sykes, and even Alfred Hitchcock—who had been a teenager during the First World War—to talk about the latest pop singles. When jazz singer Carmen McRae appeared in October 1960, she made her feelings for Roy Orbison's *Blue Angel* very clear. She told viewers she had one word for that record, and that was 'lousy'; she detested this kind of 'music'. 'But that's neither here nor there,' she said. 'I think it will be a hit because it's terrible.' Her verdict was accurate enough and hardly surprising, especially as Orbison was No. 1 at the time with his previous single *Only The Lonely*.

Younger viewers were less than satisfied with having middle-aged and sometimes patronising guests on the panel, as indeed were the artists whose records came under the microscope each week. The panellists knew little about the pop music scene and were ill-equipped to offer informed comment on the new releases. Although the BBC made tentative efforts to choose younger, trendier personalities, particularly from the mid-1960s onwards, a view persisted that the producer was still aiming the programme at this mythical teatime family audience, with parents and even grandparents as well as children watching. The BBC commissioned a report that found viewers under thirty thought most jury members on the programme didn't 'know anything about pop music, [criticised] harshly, [were] facetious, wordy, rude or ill-mannered, or [tried] to steal the show'. *Melody Maker* asked its readers to choose their ideal jury and found that Helen Shapiro and Jane Asher were proving particularly popular; the former 'was charming and she knows pop tastes', while the latter 'represented the teenage point of view and talked sense'.[12] However, David said that it was more about family entertainment than any in-depth musical analysis:

> I saw myself as the panel of a television panel game but our game was talking about gramophone records. What the panel said was not to be taken too seriously. They were often larking about and it didn't really matter what they said. Very often the person who made the record was sitting around the corner so it could be a little humiliating. Sometimes I thought the panel was completely wrong and I would say so, but I never thought that my ability to spot hits was anything special. After all, the recording managers had done that before me.[13]

Despite a preponderance of middle-aged pundits, the younger generation took over on a few shows. On 7 December 1963, at the height of Beatlemania, the panel consisted of John Lennon, Paul McCartney, George Harrison, and Ringo Starr. The weekly audience was normally around 12 million, but this time it doubled. It was transmitted live, and David was mindful of one potential difficulty.

> The noise beforehand was unbelievable. So I simply addressed the audience before the boys came on, and said, 'Look, we'd all much rather hear what The Beatles have to say rather than a lot of screaming.' And you know what? They were perfectly behaved.[14]

In July 1964, it was the turn of their rivals, The Rolling Stones, to appear—the only time there was a panel of five instead of four. Much to the delight of the popular press (if not the BBC and middle England), they cheerfully lived up to their loutish reputation. 'We just trashed every record they played,' guitarist Keith Richards recalled in his memoirs.[15] Ever the professional, Jacobs took their 'larking about' in his stride. He was particularly amused when Brian Jones turned around at one stage and told Mick Jagger, with tongue in cheek, to be quiet as he was 'spoiling Mr Jacobs' nice programme'.[16]

Juke Box Jury helped to make David Jacobs one of the most recognisable faces in broadcasting, but his fame was not all-encompassing. He once stopped for a glass of milk while driving home; as she was serving him, the proprietor's wife gave him a second look. As her husband walked in from the kitchen, she nudged him and pointed to David, saying, 'You know who this is, don't you?' He had no idea. She told him it was 'the television man'.

'I don't know what *you* want,' he told David crossly, 'I sent a cheque to your lot last week.' His wife told him that was not what she meant, and that he was the '*Juke Box* man'. He still failed to understand. 'I've told you before,' he told his wife angrily, 'and I'll not tell you again—I will *not* have one of those machines in here!' With that, he slammed back into the kitchen.[17]

On New Year's Day 1964, BBC television introduced another weekly pop show, initially for a six-week run. ITV had been airing *Thank Your Lucky Stars* for three years, and in 1963 it introduced the more hip *Ready Steady Go!*, which (unlike the first programme) would later switch to all-live performances and no miming. When the BBC launched its own television chart show, *Top of the Pops*, it was almost inevitable that producer and old friend Johnnie Stewart would ask David to be one of the four presenters. The other three were Jimmy Savile, Pete Murray, and Alan Freeman—all also Radio Luxembourg regulars—and each would host one show per month in turn. Freeman was also already established on the Light Programme with *Pick of the Pops*, having previously succeeded David as the show's regular presenter. Although Alan's animated style of presentation seemed worlds apart from David's measured, gentlemanly style, both men were good friends and respected each other as colleagues. That all the presenters were in their late thirties was not surprising. The BBC believed that experience took priority over youth and that shows that were aimed at teenagers but came under the heading of 'family entertainment' required 'mature' anchor figures.

The first show, hosted by Jimmy Savile, was an instant success, and its six-week run was extended to twelve weeks by popular demand. Reinvented and constantly transformed by several different producers in turn, it would last for forty-two years.

David was now regularly in demand as a presenter; he provided the English commentary for *A Song for Europe*, the Eurovision Song Contest, from 1957 to 1966. He also wrote an autobiography, *Jacob's Ladder*, a gentle account of his family and professional life; it was published in the summer of 1963, when he was only thirty-seven. Maybe he felt that his career in broadcasting was too good to last and it could be over as suddenly as it had begun. If this was the case, he would probably have been astonished to know that it would continue for another fifty years. Readers might regret that he did not follow it up or update it when there was an even richer past to look back on—especially as fifteen years later, with the aid of journalist Sue Freeman, he produced a short memoir, *Caroline*, about his tragically brief second marriage (see page 24).

David eventually conceded that it was time to move on, feeling that he was 'too square for the pop scene'. Although he was well-established as a broadcaster by the time rock 'n' roll came along, it was by no means his first love:

> I was never a big fan of the pop stars, preferring Frank Sinatra, Matt Monro and Petula Clark. I was the first person to play Elvis Presley, and Bill Haley and his Comets. I've never been an Elvis fan. I can see how wonderful he is, but he was never my sort of singer.[18]

In the autumn of 1966, he stepped down from *Top of the Pops*. He said the kids were getting younger and he was feeling increasingly out of place on the show: 'In a strange way I was too sophisticated for *Top of the Pops*.' He was replaced on the roster by Simon Dee, a man whose personality did not impress David: 'As a performer, he was great—but I've never known a man with more chance for success than he had—he messed it up, he really did.'[19] A man who was then making the transition from radio DJ to television chat-show host, Dee's remarkable rise and speedy fall had few parallels in the world of broadcasting.

While *Top of the Pops* had many more presenters and a long shelf life stretching out ahead, *Juke Box Jury* was less at home in an era when pop music was becoming more controversial, and it was less able to adapt to the changing times. That November, a decision to play the Mothers of Invention's 'It Can't Happen Here' led to censure from the press for playing a record that was 'recorded on a trip'.[20] What was David Jacobs doing, some wondered, allowing such a disgraceful record to be played in the name of entertainment, and why did two of the panel (perhaps with tongues in cheeks) have the audacity to vote it a hit?

The programme—by now always recorded in advance—had to fend off similar controversy a few weeks later, when the panel—fellow *Top of the Pops* presenters Pete Murray, Alan Freeman, Jimmy Savile, and Simon Dee—discussed and strongly condemned another new release, 'The Addicted Man' by The Game, a psychedelic rock number about heroin. The record and ensuing discussion were cut prior to transmission, the show was thus about seven minutes shorter, and the record was swiftly withdrawn from sale.

While David was finding himself less at home in the contemporary pop scene, he still felt obliged to defend the industry, even if his heart might not have been in it. In the spring of 1967, panellist Paul Jones—former vocalist with Manfred Mann and later a regular Radio 2 presenter himself—criticised what he called the 'depressing state' of pop music. Jacobs told him that 'some people considered the pop scene to be in unusually healthy condition'.[21]

The show was starting to look old-fashioned, and ratings were falling. In September, the reorganisation of BBC Radio took place, with the Light Programme replaced by Radios 1 and 2. At the same time, *Juke Box Jury* was moved from its regular Saturday evening slot to early Wednesday evening. In its last days, it was acknowledged that David had some choice in the records to be featured. When Georgie Fame released 'The Ballad of Bonnie and Clyde', a single inspired by (though not included in) a feature film based on the lives of the notorious gangsters, he refused to include it because of the theme of violence and lyrics referring to a victim 'lying in a pool of blood'. The rest of BBC radio and TV saw no similar need for such censorship, and, aided by heavy airplay, the record topped the chart a few weeks later. By that time, *Juke Box Jury* had been laid to rest. It went out for the last time on 27 December 1967, although it was briefly revived in 1979 and 1989 (with Noel Edmonds as chairman) and 1990 (with Jools Holland).

David was still spinning discs on the radio, presenting shows featuring easy listening and interviews with guests; these went out on Radios 1 and 2 on Sunday evenings and weekday mornings. For part of the mid-1960s, he was at the helm on *Music Through Midnight* on the Light Programme. Featuring a variety of artists and groups, guest stars, and record requests, he was one of the hosts alongside Alan Dell, Roger Moffat, and Don Moss. However, David was now ready to venture into more serious broadcasting. In April 1968, the veteran Freddie Grisewood retired as chairman of Radio 4's weekly *Any Questions?*, in which figures from public life discussed current affairs before an invited studio audience. David was one of seven people who were to audition to be Grisewood's successor, but he acquitted himself so well during the meeting that he was immediately chosen for the job. This was managed without an overwhelming vote of confidence from the first Mrs Jacobs; before he left home to chair the programme for the first time, she asked him anxiously, 'You won't ruin my favourite programme, will you?'

To at least one media critic, his new role was a positive step forward for him. One month after the show first aired, Julian Critchley, former and future Conservative MP and briefly a TV critic for *The Times*, grandly informed his readers:

> I do not like disc jockeys. The middle-men of show business, they sit profitably between pop and its public, offering as talent a brand of amiable incompetence, skilled practitioners of the art of 'chat'.

Several paragraphs later, he complimented David Jacobs on giving up his turntables for his new job, 'a metamorphosis from pop to punditry that may not lie within the compass of them all'. Meanwhile, David's former colleagues had 'no choice but to continue to play their parts as attendants on the Muse of Vulgarity'.[22]

David chaired *Any Questions?* until July 1984, and his name remained a byword for calm, courtesy, and professionalism in a show that regularly featured politicians from all political parties, senior businessmen, and trade union leaders who often held very different views. In later years, he admitted that his worst memory associated with the programme was in November 1976, when they were broadcasting from the United Reformed Church at London Road, Basingstoke. A group of local Labour Party members had been demonstrating outside against the inclusion of regular panellist Enoch Powell, former senior Conservative MP and minister and by then Ulster Unionist MP for South Down. Verbal abuse and bricks were hurled by members of the group, stained-glass windows were smashed, and the recording was suspended for about ten minutes while David led the team from the platform, returning once order was restored. It had left him, he said, 'sickened and disgusted'.[23]

Luckily, David's encounters with other politicians were more light-hearted. After the recording of one show in Southampton, he returned London on the train, sharing a compartment with Margaret Thatcher (long before she became Prime Minister) and her secretary. All three were very tired and felt the need to unwind. Fortunately, David had come well-prepared with half a bottle of Scotch. Mrs Thatcher undid the top button of her blouse, removed her shoes, and put her feet on the opposite seat as they all took it in turns to drink straight from the bottle. 'Oh dear, thank heaven my constituents can't see me now,' she sighed.

'Sorry, you're wrong,' David assured her, impressed at how unusually relaxed she looked. 'I wish they could.'[24]

A few years after becoming the chairman of *Any Questions*, David suffered two devastating tragedies in his personal life. He had married Patricia Bradlaw in 1949, and they had three daughters and a son together; however, the marriage ended in divorce in 1972. That same year, their son Jeremy, who had recently married and become a father, was killed in a car accident in Israel, where he was involved in charity work.

Within three years, David had married again, this time to Caroline. Soon afterwards, David and a pregnant Caroline were on holiday in Spain with David's friend, politician Richard Marsh, and his wife, also named Caroline. One day, David was driving his wife and friends around when they were hit by another car. The husbands were injured, but they survived; both Carolines died instantly.

David found happiness in 1979, when he married for a third time—this time to Lindsay Stuart-Hutcheson. However, in addition to losing a son and his second wife, he also had to cope with the deaths of two brothers long before their time and, worst of all, a five-year-old grandchild. On the latter occasion, he said that the seeing the pain and misery in his daughter's eyes was almost too much to bear. 'You don't get over it,' he remarked later, 'you just have to get used to it. But I've been terribly lucky in that I'm easily made to cry—in fact I still do—and I find it very refreshing.'²⁵ Moreover, all things considered, he said, 'I've had some awful things happen, but who hasn't? I've had a very lucky life and it's been so enhanced by the people who have gone. Their presence never leaves me.'²⁶

While strongly identified with the BBC at this time, with the coming of commercial radio David was ready to go elsewhere. In 1972, he had been part of the Capital Radio bid for a licence. Proposals were drafted for his aspiration to present a Sunday lunchtime show between 10.00 a.m. and 2.00 p.m.:

> ... apart from providing an appreciable music content [it] will take advantage of Mr Jacobs' talent and experience as a programme moderator. One o'clock Sunday lunchtime is traditionally the time for the family to be together and David Jacobs will direct the show towards them in a spirit which includes those listeners who are unable to enjoy the company of their own families.²⁷

The bid was unsuccessful, and Jacobs was not among the ranks of those who went on air in London the following year.

Contrary to what Julian Critchley had written, David had not completely forsaken his turntables, and he never would. Once a disc jockey, always a disc jockey, even if he and the Top 20 were now worlds apart. It was as if Radio 2 would not be Radio 2 without his reassuring presence behind the microphone, and the list of shows he presented for the station over the next few decades was a long one. From October 1971 to June 1973, he hosted the Tuesday evening edition of the hour-long *After Seven*, alternating with Michael Parkinson, Alan Freeman, Ray Moore, and Michael Aspel. Between 1974 and 1984, he presented *Melodies For You*, a show playing light classical music, and between 1978 and 1990 he presented *David Jacobs with Star Sounds*, a two-hour show on Saturday mornings. When *Sounds of the Sixties* was introduced in 1983, *Star Sounds* was dropped from the title and an hour was cut from the running time. It consisted of what he called 'our kind of music', consisting mostly of music from the era of Frank Sinatra, Bing Crosby, and Judy Garland, and from the golden age of musicals, drawn from the work of Irving Berlin, Jerome Kern, George Gershwin, and Cole Porter. One particular favourite of his, Vic Damone's version of 'The Pleasure of Your Company' (originally from the film *Royal Wedding*), was released as a single in 1983, although it never became a national hit.

When the Saturday series finished, David signed off by quoting what his mother had taught him to say when leaving a children's party: 'Thank you very much for having me. Please may I come again?'²⁸ It had, however, come to a rather messy end, being terminated by a letter that he received in the studio ten minutes before he was due to go on air. To add insult to injury, it was immediately—and publicly—announced on the BBC news at the same time. Fortunately, he had at least one ally high up in the Corporation. When told about the sacking, David Hatch, the Managing Director of Radio, was furious. He sent an angry memo around the staff, demanding to know who was responsible.

Despite this ignominious exit, it was far from the end of David's broadcasting career. Having been a nearly-man at Capital Radio, he made a brief return to independent radio in June and July 1992, when he presented weekend shows on London's Melody Radio. His producer at Melody, Gary Whitford, recalled how he would begin working on air at 6.00 a.m. and David would arrive about an hour later. During the first hour, while on air, Gary would prepare David's music, make a cup of tea, and put some biscuits out. David used the second studio and production suite to broadcast from, and after the 8.00 a.m. news, Gary would gently bring up the volume from the second studio so David could take over. Gary related that David was a lovely man and a true professional. 'He was old school, an original pioneer', but he was not one to suffer fools gladly, 'and some less respectful people found that out quite quickly'.[29]

Regarding himself mainly as a BBC man, David felt somewhat 'isolated' in his new environment, which may have explained—if not fully excused—a degree of impatience with some of those around him.

After it was over, he phoned David Hatch, telling him he wanted to come back to Radio 2, and a new slot was found for him. Between 1993 and 1998, he could be heard on *Easy Does It*, a Saturday night show featuring records and sessions from the BBC Big Band; between 1994 and 1996, David presented *Sounds Easy* on Sunday afternoons. There were also two documentary series that he narrated—*Frank Sinatra: Voice of the Century* in 1998 (in thirteen parts) and *He's Playing Our Song: The Music of Marvin Hamlisch* in 2002 (in six parts). He also made occasional appearances elsewhere, such as introducing a concert with the BBC Concert Orchestra in May 1992 (its fortieth anniversary), a seventy-fifth-birthday concert for composer and arranger Robert Farnon in 1982, and a tribute programme on Farnon's death in 2005.

On every Christmas Day morning between 1972 and 1977, David presented *Christmas Morning* on Radio 4 (later *David Jacobs' Christmas Crackers*), on which he provided the links for a helping of seasonal music and comedy clips. This spawned similar holiday shows, such as *Spring Into Summer* (airing on May bank holidays from 1976 to 1978), *Fall Into Summer*, and *The August Jacobs*. On the August bank holiday in 1977, *The Summer Show* provided a diet of music and light comedy, with sketches performed by Bernard Cribbins, Sheila Steafel, and Royce Mills.

Throughout this time, David continued to present several BBC television shows. He was chairman of a revival of *What's My Line* in 1973 and 1974 and presenter of *Where Are They Now?*, a 1979 four-part series in which he met people who had made headlines in the past, including Ruby Murray, and Sir Alec Rose. David later returned to an old role—that of the host of *Come Dancing*, his second run lasting from 1984 to 1986. After *Come Dancing*, he presented *Primetime* from 1989 to 1992, a daytime magazine show that advertised itself as aimed at the 'more mature viewer'.

His appearances on radio and TV also involved the occasional acting role. In 1974, he played himself (as the host of a 1960s award ceremony) in the rock 'n' roll nostalgia musical *Stardust*. One year later, he was cast as the host of a fictitious TV DIY programme in a Christmas Day episode of the situation comedy *Some Mothers Do 'Ave 'Em*. In the on-screen company of the accident-prone Frank Spencer (Michael Crawford), his initially unflappable demeanour gradually gave way to exasperation with Frank's not-so-wonderful new furniture and fittings, which either collapsed, blew up when switched on, or sprouted springs whenever anybody sat on them. Three decades later, David had further roles in two dramas on BBC Radio 4—as 'Jet Morgan' in *Frozen In Time*, and in the title role of *The Host*. Not forgetting his role as musical compere, albeit a self-confessed 'square', he appeared briefly on *Top of the Pops* twice again, for special editions celebrating the 1,000th show in summer 1983 and its twenty-fifth anniversary at the end of December 1988, when several of the former presenters were invited to join the current team.

Fifteen years later, in July 2003, he was one of several guests on *This Is Your Life*. On the receiving end of Michael Aspel's big red book was Bob Harris, one of Radio 2's most respected figures from the current generation. His mother had written in to *Pick of the Pops* for a dedication for him on his fifteenth birthday in April 1961. Mrs Harris and Jacobs continued to correspond, but, as he recalled in the studio that night, it was not until Bob Harris joined Radio 2 in 1997 that he realised this was the son of '*his* Mrs Harris'. He went on to pay the younger man a heartfelt accolade, telling him that he was sure his mother was very proud of him:

> [So] should all of your family be, because your dedication to music and radio is absolutely incredible. So for heaven's sake just keep on doing what you do so well and always let us have "Whispering Bob" with us.[30]

With his interest in contemporary musical theatre, David was a keen admirer of the work of Jerry Herman and his 1970s shows *Mack and Mabel* and *La Cage Aux Folles*, both of which would feature extensively in his programme. As the undisputed king of easy-listening presenters on

Radio 2, he gave his name to three compilation albums released in the 1980s—*The Saturday Side of David Jacobs* in 1983, *The Show Side of David Jacobs* a year later, and *David Jacobs At Your Request* in 1989, with a portion of the proceeds going to the Children in Need fund.

David embarked on another long-running weekend series in 1996. Over the next seventeen years, with a short interval, *The David Jacobs Collection* would act as a graceful coda to a remarkably long broadcasting career. The first series went out between 10.00 and 11.00 p.m. every Sunday evening for a twelve-month period starting in October 1996, and the second went out from 11.00 p.m. to 12.00 midnight from April 1998 onwards. It was the cue for that unmistakable voice and a friendly 'Hello there' to take his listeners through the next hour to Monday 'so that [they could] share that which many call our kind of music, all of which comes from within the David Jacobs collection'. The show opened with its signature tune, an instrumental version of Cole Porter's 'I Love You Samantha' from *High Society*, as performed by the Pete Moore Orchestra. The 'collection' comprised music from the likes of Frank Sinatra, Judy Garland, Matt Monro, Vic Damone, Ella Fitzgerald, and other easy-listening names, alongside a generous helping of musical theatre from Hollywood and Broadway. His presence every week was an oasis of reassurance in a world where so much had changed, and for listeners who could remember having been youngsters in an era when he might have been hosting *Top of the Pops,* featuring a chart and a line-up in which such disparate acts as Val Doonican and The Rolling Stones were never far apart.

Interviewed in his early seventies, David said that work was still essential to his life. He still spent two days a week at Broadcasting House, preparing his weekly shows, and in fifty-four years as a broadcaster, he had done it all—except for sports commentary. At the same time, he was touring three stage shows—*A Night in Old Vienna, Ain't She Sweet*, and *David Jacobs Goes Name-Dropping.*[31]

His services to broadcasting were recognised when he was awarded the CBE in 1996. Eleven years later, when he was eighty-one, John Clarke paid tribute in *The Times* to one of his last active contemporaries. He noted that seventy-nine-year-old Brian Matthew was still compering *Sounds of the 60s* on Radio 2 for two hours every Saturday morning, 'in an era when DJs often have a shorter shelf life than the records they're playing'. A reader promptly wrote in to correct him, asking (with tongue-in-cheek) who he thought the Sunday night presenter was—impressionist Rory Bremner, perhaps?[31] He might also have mentioned another veteran regular radio personality, Desmond Carrington, who was only four days younger but also still on Radio 2 every week. He might even have considered the career of Alan Keith, whose years of service with BBC radio had lasted from 1935 until the broadcast of his final *Your Hundred Best Tunes* in 2003, a few days after his death at the age of ninety-four.

To some of the younger, more cutting-edge radio presenters, David Jacobs was a hero whom they were glad to invite onto their shows in order to introduce the occasional record. Chris Evans stated:

> [He was] one of the cornerstones of British broadcasting in the sixties ... and a man who's still at it, a man who always has time for you, who always has something worth listening to say, the gentleman's broadcaster—may he live and broadcast forever.

Ken Bruce acknowledged that the strapline on David's weekly show was no idle boast; it definitely was 'his kind of music', because David had known most of the people whose records he played.

> [He was] suave, urbane, but he's not at all establishment, he's not at all pompous, he's not at all this friend of the great and the good although he knows them all—he's not part of that, he stands apart. He's at heart a mischief-maker and a bit of a rebel.[33]

To Lesley Douglas, a former Controller of Radio 2, he was 'everything that is wonderful about Radio 2. He has integrity, he has wit, and he has a true love of music'.[34]

He continued to work for and lend his support to various charities and community ventures over the years, as he had done throughout much of his career. This included being Life President of the Rose Theatre in Kingston-on-Thames, Vice-Patron of the Advance Centre for the Scotson Technique, and patron of Age Resource and the Disabled Photographers' Society. As a lifelong friend of Dame Vera Lynn, he was Vice-President of her charity, The Dame Vera Lynn Trust for Children with Cerebral Palsy. He was also Representative Deputy Lieutenant for the Royal Borough of Kingston. As a patron of the Stars' Organisation for Spastics, he had appeared on a novelty album in 1990, *The Spoken Word of Rock 'n' Roll*, alongside fellow supporters from the showbiz world such as Michael Aspel, Frankie Howerd, and Ronnie Corbett, as well as radio colleagues Dave Lee Travis and Noel Edmonds. He could be heard welcoming the listener to another *Juke Box Jury* on a spoken-word version of Little Richard's *Rip It Up*, though the record is arguably one that does not invite repeated listening.

Almost forty years after he became the first broadcaster to play a record by Status Quo on BBC radio, he unexpectedly came face-to-face with the group's two surviving original members, Francis Rossi and Rick Parfitt, who were paying a visit to Broadcasting House. As he looked out from a window to see them leaving, he asked if they would stop 'for one old fan', as he apologised that he had injured his ankle and was limping along 'like the old man [he tried] not to be'.

'It doesn't show on radio,' Rick assured him. Departing a few minutes later, the starstruck guitarist remarked that meeting the legendary broadcaster at long last, '*the* David Jacobs', had really made his day.[35]

David remained comparatively sprightly and active into his ninth decade. Interviewed at the age of seventy-two, he acknowledged that work was 'essential' to his life.[36] A few years later, he was still saying that he thought it was 'terrible if you can't work—you've got to do something'. Among the team at Radio 2, he was renowned as the man who might never have looked the part of a hip DJ, but naturally exuded politeness and warmth and could turn his hand to anything on radio or television. He was a friend with a wicked sense of humour, one who could tell the dirtiest of jokes in that suave style, and above all a fountain of knowledge on anything to do with musicals. Alex Lester, one of the next generation of Radio 2 presenters, once recalled having a drink in the bar with him and others, and David asked them all what their favourite musical was. When it came to Lester's turn, he had to admit he was not really familiar with any. 'Well, you would be if you listened to my fucking programme!' was the tongue-in-cheek retort.[37]

Occasionally, David's public found him to be a little too 'nice'. A listener once wrote in to Radio 2 to complain that everything David played on his show was 'superb', 'wonderful', 'marvellous', 'exciting', or 'tremendous'. David responded that he wouldn't play anything if it wasn't, because he had to sit and listen to it himself. What would be the point otherwise? He recalled the words of the late Anna Instone, one-time Head of the Gramophone Department, who had heard him present a record review show in the days of the Light Programme, when he had presented some records he did not like at all. She told him that he should not be wasting good airtime by playing anything he did not enjoy—otherwise the chances were that the listeners would not care for it either.

David celebrated his eighty-fifth birthday in May 2011, an occasion marked by a surprise party at The Ivy Restaurant in London. The party was attended by his wife, Lindsay, his family, and a guest list including songwriters Tony Hatch, Don Black, and Sir Tim Rice, broadcasting colleagues Sir Terry Wogan, Chris Evans, Pete Murray, Johnnie Walker, Tony Blackburn, and Ken Bruce, actress June Whitfield, and Dame Vera Lynn. Jazz singer and presenter Clare Teal, whose Sunday evening show on Radio 2 preceded his, was thrilled to be asked to sing at the occasion. After dinner, David stood up and spoke for twenty minutes, relating a collection of amusing anecdotes concerning some of the many well-known names from all walks of life whom he had known at various stages during his seven-decade-long career.

If not exactly a farewell, it was the last great gathering in which he took part. Parkinson's disease, liver cancer, and old age were taking their toll. Early the following year, while he was recovering from two major operations, he could still be heard each Sunday on BBC Radio 2 thanks to the broadcasting of repeats from *The David Jacobs Collection* and *Frank Sinatra: Voice of the Century*, a series he had presented in 1998 after the singer's death. He returned to his regular Sunday night slot with *The David Jacobs Collection* on 8 July, but listeners had a presentiment that his time was running out.

On 22 July 2013, David announced that he was stepping down as presenter of his show on Radio 2 on the grounds of ill health, but he intended to return for occasional appearances. His final show aired on 4 August, with the links recorded at his Sussex home earlier that week by his producer, Alan Boyd, as he was not well enough to come to the studio. At the start of the show, he announced, 'I will not stop collecting, but my sadness will be that I cannot share [the records] with all my loyal listeners. But rest assured, I will be back from time to time.' After the programme, which opened with Robert Goulet and finished with Bing Crosby, he thanked his producer, controller, and staff, without whom he could not have done it, and not least his loyal listeners. 'I hope to be spending more time with you in the not-too-distant future,' he went on. 'So until then—or whenever—it's goodnight from me, David Jacobs.'[38]

As reviewer Gillian Reynolds noted in her *Daily Telegraph* column afterwards, although the charm, the taste, the style, and the humour were still present, 'it was almost unbearably sad'.[39] In *The Jewish Chronicle*, Michael Freeland spoke for many when he said that the thought of BBC radio without the voice of Jacobs was 'almost impossible to contemplate'.[40] Many people listening must have known within their heart of hearts that it was the end of an era. A generation had grown up listening to David's voice on the radio and television, a regular feature for so long; that voice had now become little more than a frail, halting whisper, words slurred, a shadow of its former self, almost as if he was speaking to the listeners from another world altogether.

One month later, on 2 September, David Jacobs passed away at home, surrounded by his family. He was eighty-seven. The BBC director general, Tony Hall, was quick to pay tribute to 'one of the great broadcast personalities', a sentiment readily echoed by Bob Harris, Tony Blackburn, Desmond Carrington, Alex Lester, and several other fellow presenters. Among them was Clare Teal, who, at the request of his widow, Lindsay, sang 'Unforgettable' at his funeral a few days later. It was a fitting song title indeed.

2
Alan Freeman

Many a music lover has dreamed of becoming a professional artist. Tony Blair, once an aspiring rock musician, vocalist, and promoter, once said that if he could have sung like Paul Rodgers of Free and Bad Company, he might never have entered politics, let alone become Prime Minister. Some years earlier, an Australian clerk wanted to become an opera singer. His baritone voice being unequal to the task, he went into broadcasting, travelled to the other side of the world, and became one of the most eclectic disc jockeys of them all.

Born in Melbourne on 6 July 1927, Alan Leslie Freeman was the son of a timber company worker and a waitress. The younger of two brothers, he suffered from asthma and was never without an inhaler. As a child, he already gave some indication of his future musical career, as he recalled some fifty years later:

> When I was a kid back in Melbourne I always used to be a tremendous embarrassment to my parents. They would take me to the Saturday night picture show, where the adverts always had a background of orchestral music. And as soon as the music began, I would jump into the aisle and start dancing. So there I was, you see, already craving attention![1]

In his teens he was seriously overweight, and at seventeen he weighed 17 stone. A heavy smoker, he sometimes got through up to sixty cigarettes a day. Nevertheless, at one stage he thought of becoming a professional footballer. After leaving school, he joined his father's company as an assistant paymaster and accountant, but the prospect of working indefinitely in a clerical post soon palled. With his passion for music, he wanted to follow in the footsteps of the great singers. One whom he particularly idolised was the American baritone John Charles Thomas, who ironically gave vent publicly in his last years to his detestation of rock 'n' roll music. At the age of eighteen, Alan began two years of singing lessons, at the end of which he plucked up the courage to make a recording of a piece from *La traviata*. Listening to the playback was a sobering experience:

I heard myself—and I was utterly devastated. I had a very pleasant baritone voice; would I ever sing in grand opera? Pigs would fly, and that was a terrible trauma for me, because I knew how to sing, I knew how to interpret, I knew all of those things but I never had the vocal equipment. When somebody's going to be an opera singer, first of all they've got to have the basic requirements. It's got to be a good set of vocal chords, because if it's not, it's dull as dishwater. And I didn't just want to be an opera singer, I wanted to be the best baritone the world had ever heard. It was sad—it was a great let-down for me.[2]

His teacher sweetened the pill by telling him that he had 'a very good baritone voice that flowed', but he knew that a career as a professional opera singer would be beyond him.

A career as a music presenter in broadcasting would therefore be the next best thing. In 1951, a friend working in commercial radio in Melbourne suggested that he should audition as an announcer, and he joined Station 7LA in Tasmania. This was in the early days of radio broadcasting, when continuity announcers were employed as presenters of musical programmes incorporating opera, ballet, classical music, and of the hit parade, featuring discs by Rosemary Clooney, Kay Starr, Peggy Lee, and Guy Mitchell. They might also be asked to double as newsreaders, quizmasters, and readers of commercials. Returning to mainland Australia, he worked in an all-night station, 3AK, The Voice of The Night, from 12.00 midnight to 7 a.m. He could be assured of at least one devoted listener and fan—his mother. One night he played a Frank Sinatra album and then nodded off. At about 2.30 a.m., the studio phone woke him up. 'Hello,' he answered sleepily. 'Dear, I think it's finished,' his mother informed him. Within a few days he was fired.

Nevertheless, he found another job at Melbourne 3KZ, The Brighter Broadcasting Service, where he stayed until 1957, by which time he was engaged to be married. Several of his colleagues in Australia were travelling abroad and writing back to him to say how wonderful it was overseas. A friend who had gone on to find employment in commercial television in London tried to put him off, telling him not to try and come to work in England's capital city as it was the centre of showbiz, if not the centre of the world, 'and [he would] never get it—because [he didn't] have the talent'. Despite his reasonably safe job with 3KZ, Alan refused to be put off, feeling that he needed to take a chance at this point in his career, especially as it might not come again. His fiancée, a model, delivered him an ultimatum—either he went on his trip around the world or they got married, but he could not do both. He chose the former, but promised he would keep in touch. He met her again on a brief return to Australia, by which time she was happily married to someone else.

Alan sailed from Port Norman in April 1957, with a return ticket to Australia in his pocket. With the agreement of his employers, he was making a nine-month trip around the world, promising to return to Melbourne by January 1958. Once he had arrived in London, he decided he did not need to go back. On reaching St Pancras Station, he got out of the train and hailed a cab for Big Ben. As they approached Parliament Square, looking at the double-decker red buses, the black taxis, and the Houses of Parliament, he said to himself with amazement, 'It's all real!' As he got out, Big Ben struck, and he burst into tears 'out of total patriotism'. Almost at once he felt that he did not care about the job from which he had been granted a leave of absence—he wanted to stay in England and would even take a job selling shirts if nothing better came up. He sent his employer letters of delay while making his mind up, but these were soon followed by one of resignation. He had found his new home, and it was not as a shirt salesman.

To begin with, Alan was totally impressed with what he discovered, in particular the rather demure style of music presentation on radio. Turning on the Light Programme, he would hear a BBC announcer intone solemnly after a piece of music that listeners had just heard Frank Sinatra on a new gramophone record, singing 'Come Fly With Me'. Alan later recalled, 'I fell off my chair laughing, and I thought to myself, it's all a little too gentle! Of course he was on a gramophone record!'[3] Although Christopher Stone had been the first radio announcer and presenter of music on the BBC in 1927, the term 'disc jockey' was not coined until 1935 and even then generally only used in America. It was a concept that would take a few years to catch on in Britain, initially only in a few dance halls up and down the country, and also on the airwaves of Radio Luxembourg.

The world—or, rather, London—was his oyster. After going to a few parties in the capital, he met a radio announcer and told him he was seeking employment. A few days later, his contact told him that Radio Luxembourg, for which so many of the shows were recorded in London, was looking for summer relief announcers, so it might pay to give them a try. The bosses offered him an audition in the studio and called back two days later to say they had heard his tape and thought it was adequate. From that came an offer of three months' work at a rate of £25 per week. It was the foot in the door that Alan needed, and he continued to present late-evening programmes there until the early 1970s. At this stage the BBC had its personalities, celebrities, and duty announcers, while Radio Luxembourg had station hosts and resident announcers. Television had its masters of ceremonies or comperes, but the idea of the DJ had not yet arrived in Britain.

At the dawn of the 1960s, Great Britain was a nation in which teenagers and young adults had significant spending power, though without the full extent of consumer choice that would be available within a few years. Alan had the good fortune to be in the right place at the right time, and to be one of the first to cater for the demand. Yet Britain was still somewhat behind the times. There was as yet no commercial radio based in Britain, and despite the explosion of rock 'n' roll music in the 1950s, airtime for the new sounds was limited. BBC record programmes were severely restricted by a Musicians' Union 'needle time' agreement. The Light Programme was only playing an hour or two of new vinyl releases—nowhere near sufficient to keep up with the output of the major record labels. Apart from *Pick of the Pops*, *Saturday Club* (hosted by Brian Matthew), and *Easy Beat* on Sunday morning (presented initially by Matthew and later by Keith Fordyce), there was little opportunity to hear the latest hit records. One had to rely on the English service of Radio Luxembourg, which was limited to broadcasting eight hours a day from 6.00 p.m., or, from the early 1960s, the offshore pirate stations—both with poor reception. For most consumer goods, wartime rationing was now but a memory, but the broadcasting of pop records was still heavily restricted. If people wished to hear those they had not already purchased (and therefore probably did not know whether they would like them or not), the only alternative was the nearest jukebox. It was a vacuum that Radio Caroline and the other pirates were eager to fill, thus forcing the government and the Corporation to give serious consideration to national policy.

If Christopher Stone was the grandfather of British DJing, Jack Jackson was the father. A musician (fiddle, cello and trumpet) in the 1920s dance band era, he made the transition from musician to music presenter with a record show on Radio Luxembourg in the late 1930s, joining the BBC Light Programme in 1948. He went on to host *Housewives' Choice* and *Record Round-Up* in a career that lasted until 1968, up to and including the early months, when Radio 1 and Radio 2 were still combined for part of the evening. But for ill-health and retirement in 1973 and his death five years later at the age of seventy-one, he might have endeared himself to younger generations of listeners. It fell to Alan Freeman to pick up the baton and leave his mark on music broadcasting into the new millennium.

For some years, Alan's airtime hours per week on Radio Luxembourg amounted to three or four times as many as those on his Light Programme output, which consisted of just one hour. Although he was always regarded as a BBC name, at the start of his career in Britain he was really a London-based Luxembourg presenter better-known for his radio and TV appearances with the BBC. Several presenters worked simultaneously for the Corporation (or as ITV continuity announcers) and the Grand Duchy station. The latter was a valuable source of additional income, and the BBC, which offered DJs very limited work for a few hours a week at best, could not afford enough to offer exclusive contracts. The two stations thus shared a pool of freelance names working simultaneously for both, among them Jimmy Savile, Jack Jackson, Pete Murray, David Jacobs, Keith Fordyce, Brian Matthew, Jimmy Young, and Jean Metcalfe. As far as the BBC was concerned, they were working for Radio Luxembourg 'in a different capacity' and there was no question of a conflict of interest. Jack Jackson recorded his Luxembourg and BBC shows at his own studio in the Canary Isles every week and posted both tapes to his London agent in the same packet. If his agent was not available, the package for Luxembourg was sent to their London studios in Hertford Street and the BBC copy was delivered to Portland Place.

Alan was the ultimate perfectionist. His pre-recorded Luxembourg show, the five-nights-a-week *Pops Till Midnight*, was done in three or four takes. From the start of his career in Britain, he worked with his producer to ensure that any programme to which he put his name would consist of carefully selected music and sympathetically chosen signature tunes, musical 'links and bridges', and chart countdowns musically in key with their surroundings. On his Luxembourg shows, which lasted until the early 1970s, all the commercials were carefully arranged in harmony with the surrounding music. With the advent of British commercial radio, its counterpart in the European Grand Duchy would eventually be eclipsed, but for many years it had no competition and was essential teenage listening.

When Alan joined the BBC, it was the start of a career that would endure for forty years (with short breaks working for other stations). In 1960, he joined the Light Programme as a presenter of *Housewives' Choice*, later hosting *Twelve O'Clock Spin*, and in January 1961 he took over a new show, *Records Around Five*. The latter was introduced by his signature tune, 'At The Sign of the Swingin' Cymbals', which had been recommended by producer and future Radio 1 Controller Derek Chinnery. It was released in 1960 by Parlophone on a single credited to Brian Fahey (the composer) and his Orchestra. Two years later, it was reissued on the same label as 'At The Sign of the Swingin' Cymbal' by Brian Faye and his Orchestra. In 1970, a slightly faster version was recorded by Brass Incorporated with yet another minor title change—'At The Sign of the Swinging Cymbal'—and released on Pye International.

In September 1961, David Jacobs handed *Pick Of The Pops* over to Alan. At the time it was part of a longer Saturday evening show, *Trad Tavern*. 'Trad was happening and I loved the music,' he recalled:

> David Jacobs was presenting *Pick of the Pops* and they wanted to incorporate that into *Trad Tavern*, a live show with an audience. David

didn't care for standing up in front of a jazz audience, so I was asked to do it. It was a three-hour programme and there were three segments of *Pick of the Pops*. It was a suit, collar and tie job for me and all the jazz freaks wondered who I was![4]

The show saw the genesis of the catchphrases with which Freeman would always be identified. 'Hi there, pop-pickers!' was the first. When asked about the phrase some years later, he explained that it sounded better than merely referring to or greeting his listeners as 'ladies and gentlemen'. The latter was not only boring, but blatantly obvious, as all his listeners were bound to be ladies and gentlemen anyway. Why not call them 'pop-pickers' instead? Soon afterwards came the inimitable 'Er … not 'alf!', and a regular signing-off, 'All right? Stay bright!' At least one of these came about almost by accident. According to one source, he used to tell the story that soon after moving to London, he was telephoning a friend in Australia, and finished off the conversation with 'Talk to you tomorrow, all right?' Almost at once, she phoned back.

'What did you say just now?'

'All right!' he replied.

'That's amazing—so catchy,' she said. 'You should use it!'[5] Another source suggests that the person responsible for his using the phrase was actress Ann Todd, a neighbour in the same block of flats in London.

Above all there was the nickname 'Fluff', bestowed on him because of a favourite white submarine sweater. Partly filled with oil for warmth, it gradually became more black and grimy as time wore on. Anxious that it would not wash properly but loath to part with it, Alan kept it until it got even more disreputable and had to be cleaned. When it came back, it looked more like a sheep than a pullover. Wearing it as he walked into a party one evening, a friend greeted him with, 'Bloody hell, it's fluffy Freeman!'

For some listeners, Alan's style was an acquired taste, and maybe a little too ahead of its time. However, the first in their field do not always have an easy ride to public acceptance. With all due respect to David Jacobs, it was left to his successor to grab the show by the scruff of the neck. Tony Blackburn was a teenager at this point, but he was destined to become the presenter of a revamped *Pick of the Pops* on BBC Radio 2 half a century later; he readily acknowledged that the programme was almost the BBC's only concession to pop radio, and 'Freeman taught the British how to do it'. Moving from Saturday night to a Sunday afternoon slot, it was a regular standalone item on the schedules from April 1962. Some listeners complained about Alan's presentation, and the BBC bosses bowed to their indignation by asking David to make a brief return towards the end of the year, while Don Moss was the host for a few weeks in the autumn of 1963.

Yet Alan was impossible to keep down, and he came back to *Pick of the Pops* every week for the next ten years, until September 1972.

Although his delivery sounded spontaneous, it was generally the result of painstaking preparation. In 1967, during the early days of Radio 1, Tony Blackburn was astonished to see a script for *Pick of the Pops* on his desk with 'ums', 'aaahs', and 'number errrs' written in. How much the hesitations were scripted, it is hard to be sure. Jon Myer, who was at Capital Radio for fourteen years and worked as Alan's producer at Capital before becoming music manager at BBC Radio 6 Music, recalled that Alan often used pauses and catchphrases to cover up the fact that he was never the slickest operator of the studio desk, not always being certain which button or fader to use. While saying something on air along the lines of, 'Er, music lovers, I think we'll go along with, er, this,' he would be trying to figure out which fader to push up. Nevertheless, he always meticulously rehearsed the chart rundown for the end of *Pick of the Pops* in its various forms, and he made extensive notes as to where he should be in his script for each of the musical stabs.

During one of his breaks from the show, Alan was asked to present *Pop To Bed*, a thirty-minute slot broadcast between 11.30 p.m. and 12.00 midnight, alternating with Pete Murray and Alan Dell. Anna Instone, the Head of Gramophone Programmes, told him that he had to play 'soft ballads' during the twenty minutes before midnight—in other words, two-thirds of the show—as that was when listeners went to bed. He answered defiantly, 'Miss Instone, when Alan Freeman is on the air, nobody goes to bed.' A producer later told him that he was not allowed to say 'Alan Freeman says pop to bed' on the radio on the grounds that it was not appropriate; Alan told him that it was his show and he would say what he liked.

As the first BBC presentation of the weekly chart, *Pick of the Pops* was an instant success, with listeners never having heard anything like it on British radio before. Alan divided it into four 'units'. 'Unit One' began the show with a selection of new releases, while 'Unit Two' played records from the lower 'hit parade' rankings; 'Unit Three' was a short (one-track) LP spot. 'Unit Four' was the climax, covering the second half-hour of the show, with the 'Top Ten' played in ascending order from No. 10 up to a climactic end-of-show play for the week's No. 1, followed by an almost breathless countdown of the Top 20 over the signature tune. Add to that his endearing patter and stock catchphrases, and the result was little short of revolutionary at the time. For one hour every week, Alan was a friend to millions of listeners as he lifted the lid on the hit parade. The show became almost compulsory listening for any children or teenagers within striking distance of a radio, especially in a world in which everything else on a Sunday was closed.

Alan also recorded a one-off single himself. 'Madison Time', on which he called out a series of dance instructions to the accompaniment of a jazz tune performed by The Talmy Stone Band, appeared on the Decca label in November 1962 but failed to chart, as had a version by Jimmy Savile and The Vernons Girls two years earlier. More successful were his occasional ventures into television. He had been a regular member of the panel on *Juke Box Jury*; in January 1964, he and David Jacobs were obvious choices for the original team of presenters for *Top of the Pops* on TV, remaining there for five years. In 1963, he took over as compere of *Go Man Go*, a big-band and pop show on the Light Programme, which came to an end soon afterwards.

Back on the radio, his theme tunes and jingles, once heard, were never forgotten. 'At the Sign of the Swinging Cymbal' was replaced in 1966 for four years by The Harry Roberts Sound's 'Quite Beside the Point', another jazz-pop tune featuring brass, harpsichord, and flute. A new version of the old tune was later reinstated.

Radio Luxembourg already had a weekly hit parade show, but theirs had been a relatively tame affair. The whole countdown format, featuring competition between the week's best-selling singles and the ultimate prize of the week's No. 1, was something new entirely. Alan's boyish excitement was almost infectious as he tried to forecast which records would overtake each other, to say nothing of his eager speculation as to which had the best chance of going all the way to the top. Many a disbelieving parent must have shaken his or her head, muttering, 'Does it really matter?' Yes, dear parent—it did. It mattered to the record industry, of course, but also drew in an eager community of young listeners up and down the land in a ritual that they could genuinely call their own.

One teenager who tuned in regularly was Ian Gillan, who grew up listening on the radio under his pillow:

> He became enormously famous for his presentation of the charts and the way in which he would do his rundown of the Top 20. It appeared as if it was extremely stylish, but it really was the embodiment of Freeman's enthusiasm for the music he played. There never was before in rock music, pop music, and there hasn't been since, anyone who presents the songs as if everyone is really important ... He's an ultra-professional presenter and the great thing is he's been able to avoid dominating the proceedings when so many other people fall into the trap. He talks from the heart and he's got a fantastic speaking voice—an integral part of rock 'n' roll.[6]

In the late 1960s, Alan was a champion of Ian's first major group, Episode Six, a well-respected five-piece who recorded several Radio 1 sessions, played live at the Radio 1 club, and released a number of singles that never quite made the chart. The most notable of these were a cover of The Beatles' 'Here, There and Everywhere' and a fast-paced rock-meets-classics instrumental, 'Mozart Versus the Rest', inspired by the recent success of Love Sculpture's 'Sabre Dance'. Alan, he wrote later, 'was brilliant' to them. Every time they brought out a new 45, the other DJs were full of the 'Hello, dear boy, I do like your record,' but 'Fluff' would actually play it.[7] Ian and Episode Six's bass guitarist, Roger Glover, left the group and joined Deep Purple in 1969. Alan was among those who enthusiastically attended their first live performance in 1970, keyboard player Jon Lord's *Concerto for Group and Orchestra*; a ground-breaking fusion of hard rock and classical music, it reflected the styles of music with which Alan would be associated as a presenter.

In 1964, at the height of Beatlemania, Alan was asked by producer Bryant Marriott if he would present a couple of Bank Holiday specials, *From Us To You*, featuring The Beatles. These included the group playing some of their songs and a handful of cover versions, reading out listeners' dedications, and enjoying some banter with the presenter. Their freshness and spontaneity had appealed greatly to Alan from the start. While working with them—and it hardly felt like work at all—he recalled that he felt like a kid again, and he told Paul McCartney that they 'salvaged him from middle age'.

When the pirate radio stations were closed down by the government in the summer of 1967, BBC Radio underwent a complete facelift. The Light Programme became Radio 2, a station for the older musical listener, the Third Programme was replaced by Radio 3, and the Home Service was replaced by Radio 4. Radio 1, the new youth music station, employed several of the former pirate DJs. Although he was several years older than them, the forty-year-old yet seemingly ageless Alan Freeman was happy to take his place alongside the pirate DJs, presenting a newly expanded, two-hour *Pick of the Pops* every Sunday afternoon. For any teenager or young adult with an interest in the pop scene, it remained essential listening. Until then, music radio, still an evolving form, had in the main comprised a sequence of gramophone records, the titles and artists being voiced by 'resident announcers', some of whom had little interest in the records themselves. The presence of knowledgeable and enthusiastic presenters such as Alan and John Peel (at the other end of the musical spectrum) helped to transform popular music from something more or less disposable into an art form deserving of more serious consideration.

On 5 January 1968, a week after *Juke Box Jury* had come to the end of its eight-year run, *All Systems Freeman* was launched on BBC1. Shown on Friday evenings, it ran for twelve weeks. The set was arranged like a radio station, with Alan sitting at a console with two visible turntables that were not merely props but provided genuine audio input. He was seen wearing headphones ('cans'), and doing his own vision mixing on a panel adjacent to his turntables, controlling the musical inserts with sliders and dials. The programme included appearances from groups and acts such as Engelbert Humperdinck, Herman's Hermits, The Move, and The Spencer Davis Group in the studio and on film, alongside comment and opinion on the pop scene. It was popular at the time, but as it was scheduled early in the evening and with family audiences in mind (like *Top of the Pops*), it was thought by some that the show could not attain the ratings that a more discerning teenage audience would have given it later in the evening. This was fixed three or four years later with *The Old Grey Whistle Test*.

At around the same time, Alan was invited to write the occasional album sleeve note for an artist or genre with whom he was especially glad to be associated. In the summer of 1967, he penned a lively, tongue-in-cheek endorsement for Simon Dupree and the Big Sound's debut album *Without Reservation*, in which he declared 'that it was only a matter of time before they'd have the pop record buying public at their feet'. He was almost proved right, for the group achieved the unusual feat of having a Top 40 album before a hit single; the latter dream was realised when 'Kites' reached the Top 10 at the end of the year.

Some two years later, Alan demonstrated his passion for Tamla Motown by playing many reissued singles on *Pick of the Pops*; the singles had sold poorly in the mid-1960s, when they were first released, but they performed more strongly towards the end of the decade. Alan's commitment to Motown was saluted when he was asked to contribute a few thoughts to be printed on the sleeve of *Motown Chartbusters Vol. 3*, which he praised as 'a pretty tremendous album'. The public agreed with him, for early in 1970 the package, encased in a particularly light-sensitive, eye-catching silver design, became the first various-artists compilation to top the British album charts. He had been responsible for rescuing at least one track on it from semi-obscurity; in 1964, Martha and the Vandellas' 'Dancing in the Street' had only just made the British Top 30. Once the music of Motown caught on in a bigger way in Britain, it was one of several records on the label to be reissued about four years later, now credited to Martha Reeves and the Vandellas. Alan had such a passion for the record that he made a point of playing it on his Radio Luxembourg show every night at the same time, and the result was a top five hit. Some of his fellow presenters admitted that they were grateful that it had become such a success at last—now that so many people had purchased it, he would have no need to play it again so regularly.

The era when disc jockeys on the radio would be taken seriously by the media at large was still some way ahead. From time to time, the weightier end of the press would regularly feature comments on what superior writers dismissed as the inane standard of babbling by young presenters evidently far too fond of the sound of their own voices. They also had the additional handicap in that Radio 1 was the government-approved answer to pirate radio, and it would therefore always be derided by critics anxious to proclaim their street credibility. In an interview around the time of Radio 1's tenth anniversary, Alan succinctly put it:

> You see, it was the successor to the pirates and so from its inception it was unglamorous because it wasn't illegal. And some of the disc-jockeys who had been pirates lost a bit of their glamour because they suddenly became legal and respectable.[8]

While some DJs undoubtedly regarded themselves as 'personalities' who might be better fitted to stand-up comedy, others had that gift of communicating their passion for the music they played to their listeners. Alan's ebullient, outgoing delivery and catchphrases—even an endearing sense of self-parody—never masked his love for many of the records he featured. As a presenter, his job was to feature records from the charts every week, apart from those which were banned by the BBC on the grounds of dubious taste or vulgarity. There were inevitably several records not to his personal taste, but he took them all in his stride, resisting the temptation to pass adverse comment on anything he did not like. This principle was that when a presenter played a record, he or she was under an obligation not to score cheap points by being dismissive or making 'smart remarks' for the fun of it, and thus literally 'playing with someone's future'. As he admitted, no chart-show DJ could play the Top 20 and tell the British public that a record that had sold in its thousands was awful, nor imply that those who had bought it were wrong—even if he personally disliked it. He later stated that one of the worst singles he had ever heard was 'Grandad', a children's novelty song by actor Clive Dunn, who was best known as 'Corporal Jones' in the TV situation comedy series *Dad's Army*. It topped the charts in January 1971 and sold 3 million copies; 'Who's right and who's wrong?' Alan asked.[9]

A few years down the line, Alan and his colleagues would have more say in what he spun on the turntables, and sometimes he would be given the freedom to champion records that he felt really deserved success. In October 1971, Argent's 'Hold Your Head Up' was released as a single, with a full six-minute version being replaced by a shorter, more radio-friendly edit early the next year. Alan adored the record, played it week after week, and was delighted when it eventually entered the charts and climbed to No. 5. Although Led Zeppelin were one of the few acts who refused to let their record label release any of their album tracks as singles in Britain, this did not prevent Alan, their most devout champion on radio, from the occasional airing of certain tracks. To their guitarist, Jimmy Page, it was as if Alan was the only person on the BBC who was playing Led Zeppelin; the group was always an 'albums band' at a time when it was almost impossible for a group who did not issue singles to be featured on daytime radio.

> He was the one who was calling us up when we were finishing an album. When's it coming out? When can I have something to play? He enjoys and believes in what he is doing and that's what comes through about him, provided you've always got conviction—that's what's going to tell at the end of the day with the public.[10]

Alan remained Mr Chart Rundown on Radio 1 for several years. During one broadcast, he was holding a piece of paper that listed the new chart, about to reveal all to several million listeners worldwide, when his colleague, Dave Lee Travis, entered the studio. Dave took a box of matches out of his pocket, lit a match, and set fire to the paper. Instead of panicking, Alan held the paper gingerly by the corner and, as the flame started to lick around it, memorised the higher positions, enabling him to read the last few at the final moment, as a wisp of brown ash fluttered onto the desk in front of him.

From time to time, Alan was offered small roles on the big screen, generally playing himself. Two musical comedies—*It's Trad, Dad!* in 1962 and *Just For Fun* a year later—saw him and David Jacobs in small walk-on parts alongside various British and American pop and jazz performers. He found himself in more serious territory in Peter Cushing's *Dr Terror's House of Horrors* in 1965 and Dirk Bogarde's *Sebastian* in 1968. In 1986, he had the role of 'Call-me-Cobber' in an adaptation of Colin MacInnes's *Absolute Beginners*, set in late-1950s London, starring Patsy Kensit. He also had a part as a doctor in the 1992 drama *Passionata*. Like many other media celebrities, he sometimes did voiceovers in television adverts—for Omo washing powder, Gordon Moore's Cosmetic Toothpaste, and most notably for Brentford Nylons. For a brief period during the mid-1970s, his name was almost synonymous with the latter, and at a *Melody Maker* Poll Awards party, Peter Cook once introduced him with the words, 'And here comes Alan Freeman—wearing his Brentford Nylons!' An accomplished pianist, he sometimes gave friends and guests at home private recitals of operatic and jazz favourites.

In addition to his regular Sunday afternoon slot, in April 1972 he began a daily show on Radio 1. For fourteen months, he could be heard between 3.00 p.m. and 5.00 p.m. every weekday, with 'Soul Bossa Nova' by Quincy Jones as his theme tune. The show initially overlapped with *Pick of the Pops*, which finished for a while at the end of September 1972 and was replaced by *Solid Gold Sixty*, a three-hour chart show on Sundays with a new format and presenter, Tom Browne.

This was to be a period of considerable and very diverse broadcasting activity for Alan. In 1973, Radio 1 producer Johnny Beerling devised *The Radio 1 Roadshow*, a travelling event that was broadcast live from various seaside locations around the country every summer for about eight weeks. Freeman hosted the first, which took place in Newquay on 23 July. At the same time, he narrated a Radio 1 series, *The Story of Pop*, written by Tim Blackmore and Charlie Gillett. Beginning with Teresa Brewer's 'Music Music Music' and Bill Haley and His Comets' 'Rock Around The Clock', it presented a full musical history (up to the present day) in fifty-two parts and spawned a double album featuring forty hits from 1951 to 1967. Shortly afterwards, the station devised another new series, *Quiz Kid*, of which Alan was the first host. It was recorded at various youth and boys' clubs. Freeman particularly enjoyed being in the chair as he was always keen to do his bit for charity. He had a particular interest in working for children with special needs and championing relevant organisations, and he was Vice-President of the London Association of Youth Clubs.

However, the venture with which Alan would always be associated with, almost as much as *Pick of the Pops*, was the *Saturday Rock Show*. The Radio 1 management had long wanted to launch a regular specialist programme with a spotlight on heavy and progressive rock. One day, producer Derek Chinnery called him into the office to pick his brains on the 'strange jingles' and 'rock music' to which he seemed so attached. An offer was promptly made to Alan to host a two-hour show at the weekend, with *carte blanche* to play exactly what he wanted. His enthusiasm was short-lived at first. When he was told that it would be on Saturday afternoons, his 'world fell apart, because at that particular stage it was the gutter as far as ratings went', and he feared it was one step away from being pensioned off from the station altogether.

Luckily for Alan, he had a sympathetic, like-minded producer in Tony Wilson, not to mention thousands of eager fans who had been longing for something of the kind. He embraced it with his customary zeal, and for fans it became another must-hear show, regularly topping music press polls as the best show on radio. Regular helpings of Genesis, Pink Floyd, Deep Purple, Yes, King Crimson, Black Sabbath, Bob Dylan, Caravan, Status Quo, and Emerson, Lake and Palmer—including lengthy tracks, a definite no-no for daytime radio—could be guaranteed, as was a weekly rundown of the rock album chart and the first airing of those glorious classics-meets-hard rock jingles. A few seconds of Elton John's 'Saturday Night's Alright (For Fighting)' would inevitably be aired near the start of the show each week. Now that the accent was on rock and not pop, the verbal welcome underwent a subtle change—'Greetings, music lovers!'

The jingles became ever more eclectic, breaking new ground. Saturday afternoon listeners would be greeted with a burst of 'Welcome Back My Friends to the Show That Never Ends...', taken from the beginning of a live album of the same title by Emerson, Lake and Palmer. This segued into a few seconds of The Edgar Winter Group's 'Frankenstein' and then a few bars from one of Dvorak's Slavonic Dances. Later variations on the theme would interpolate some of these with snatches of AC/DC's 'For Those About To Rock (We Salute You)', Handel's 'Hallelujah Chorus', Rainbow's 'Long Live Rock 'n' Roll', and Bizet's 'March of the Toreadors'. There might also be a few seconds of 'The William Tell Overture', 'Land of Hope and Glory', and the distinctive-yet-unnamed guitar chord that famously opened The Beatles' 'A Hard Day's Night'. At a time when most radio jingles were downright corny, cheesy, and irritating after a few hearings, there remained something timeless about the quality of Alan's magnificently grandiose sound collages of classics and hard rock. In a way it was quite logical, as little imagination was required to make a connection between some of the more bombastic compositions (in the best possible sense) of nineteenth-century composers such as Wagner and Tchaikovsky, and the unashamedly classically influenced work of Deep Purple and Emerson, Lake and Palmer. A few years later, when classical musicians and performers were asked to name their favourite rock artists, they would almost invariably place the likes of Meat Loaf and Queen high on their list; Queen's vocalist, Freddie Mercury, once recorded an album of duets with opera singer Montserrat Caballe. In the notes to a compilation album towards the end of his long career, Alan noted:

> It's a pity when people suggest that if you play rock music, you shouldn't play classical. And what a shame to say 'if you like this type of music, you can't like that'. If it's a good tune, and you enjoy it—then play it! This is why between Jethro Tull and Jimi Hendrix on the *Rock Show* you might catch a short burst of Nigel Kennedy giving it a bit of the old fiddle.[11]

The respect that so many performers had for Alan was confirmed with the release of a compilation double album in 1976, *By Invitation Only*. Issued on the Atlantic label, the eighteen tracks included an eclectic selection of music from their catalogue, including Yes, The Pretty Things, Buffalo

Springfield, The Rolling Stones, Led Zeppelin, and Aretha Franklin. It was personally compiled by Alan after he had secured permission from each of the acts in turn, as shown by handwritten replies included on the inner section of the gatefold sleeve.

Despite this, Alan remained disarmingly down to earth, seeing his role rather like that of a public servant, constantly reminding himself that he was not being paid just to amuse himself, but to amuse and entertain the listeners:

> I would like to think that I am Alan Freeman, the Power and the Glory, Amen, but I can't—because I really am not, you see. The best I can do really is to run a pretty mediocre last to the worst record I might ever play. The music is the important thing. No one is indispensable. If I were to die today the Saturday programmes [the *Rock Show* on Radio 1] would still go on the air. I might be missed, but not for long.[12]

When punk rock stormed the front pages of the tabloids from the end of 1976 onwards, he invited listeners to write in and say whether there was a place in the programme for the Sex Pistols, The Stranglers, and others. Fans were more or less split down the middle, but Alan Freeman proved that there was a place for everything by including punk and new wave alongside classic hard and progressive rock. Chris Tarrant, who would later be a colleague of his on Capital Radio, put his finger on it perfectly:

> He clearly loves every musical change of direction, every switch over decades, he seems to be completely at home in it as much as in the last one, and there have been so many of them in Fluff's long career. He's never ever sounded remotely dated. His knowledge of the subject is massive and there is a real joy in him doing his work that has always shone through. He's done a tremendous amount for years and years, developing talent in the music industry on air. He clearly has a huge enthusiasm and love for the music he's playing and, equally important, for the people who made it. I also can't think of anybody who's ever had a bad word to say about Fluff. Everybody loves him—he is ageless, he is unique, he's probably the best there's ever been.[13]

Much mourned by listeners, the *Rock Show* came to an end in the summer of 1978. Alan tried to make light of the show's demise in public, looking back on nearly two decades as a DJ at the BBC. In an interview, he said he was sometimes surprised that he had lasted so long:

> The only explanation I can offer is that I have always given great attention to the way a programme moves—to evolving musical patterns

which hold the listeners' interest. When I sit at the turntable I am involved in a series of love affairs. I am in love with each record as it comes up. I enjoy the feeling of being done with the record I am playing. Music is not just my job. It is my life. From the time of my first musical crush—an Italian opera singer, Toti Dalmonte—I have loved all music from opera to rock.[14]

The decision had not come from Alan himself, but from Derek Chinnery, now Radio 1 Programme Controller, who said he thought it wrong for a peak-time slot to be taken up by what he believed was a minority taste in music. Nothing should last forever, he said, and it was time a younger presenter or another genre of music (or both) should be given a chance. Alan was acknowledged as one of the medium's most respected presenters; he had attracted a devoted audience and delivered excellent listening figures for the previous five years, winning reader's polls in the music papers year after year while also being saluted by the artists whose music he championed so eloquently. However, this appeared to count for little. Justifiably dismayed (if not angered) by the decision, he left Radio 1 at the end of August and went into 'the wilderness' for some time. He was in demand for personal disco appearances and the like, but such a role was hardly an appropriate use of his talents.

For the first time in almost two decades, the unthinkable had occurred. Alan Freeman, so long the cornerstone of popular music on the Light Programme and then on Radio 1, was no longer to be heard at the touch of a transistor switch and the turn of a dial. Still, there was no exiling a man with his energy and personality from the airwaves for long. Tim Blackmore had joined Capital Radio and invited Alan to sit in for their regular rock show presenter, Nicky Horne, while he was on holiday. It was effectively Capital's answer to what had been Alan's own slot on Radio 1. Delighted to be on air again, Alan filled the temporary position so well that Aidan Day, Head of Music at Capital, asked him to stay on. After finishing what he thought would be his last show, Tim and Aidan found him packing his cartridges away and asked him what on earth he was doing. When he told them he was going, they told him, to his delight, that he was going nowhere. He was asked to present the Top 40 of the decade on New Year's Eve, and a decision was taken to revive his old Radio 1 programme as *Pick of the Pops Take 2*, combining the week's current Top 15 with a corresponding chart from the same week of an earlier year.

When he was asked in an interview why he had left his old broadcasting home for the commercial sector, he made the best of the situation while concealing the real reason. His reply was loyalty itself, even if there was a gentle dig at the Corporation. He said he felt the need to breathe again, to go out in the street and see what was happening in the world outside. Delighted as he was at having been there on a national basis for twenty years, he stated that when he was 'so safely employed by the BBC', he really was 'very much cocooned'. When he was invited to Capital, he went over, they talked, and they offered him a job, which he was very happy to accept. 'Capital is very different to the BBC,' he said, 'because the BBC is a little more stiff, more staid—here it's all very much a family affair.'[15]

Television nostalgia beckoned again when *Juke Box Jury* was revived for a ten-week run in June 1979, with Noel Edmonds in the chair. Alan returned as a panellist on one programme, alongside Elaine Paige, Joan Collins, and Johnny Rotten. True to form, the punk rock icon scowled throughout the show and lived up to his image by panning every record played. While they were discussing The Monks' 'I Ain't Gettin' Any', he and Alan began to argue and the latter calmly told him to shut up. Johnny appeared to take it in good heart, although he got up and walked off shortly before the end of the show.

Soon after Tim Blackmore left Capital in 1983, Alan—always the most apologetic man on the planet—rang him to say, 'I miss our conversations but I don't like picking your brains—or rather, I feel guilty about taking up your time.' The dilemma about not paying Tim for his advice was soon resolved. 'You be my manager,' Alan said. 'When people ask me to do things, you say yes or no.' A gentleman's agreement was accordingly made—neither man wanted a contract—and Blackmore remained his manager for the rest of his life.

As he entered his sixties, Alan's love of playing records on the radio was undiminished:

> If you're not enjoying it, and in some way communicating that excitement or that love of it all to an audience, you mustn't be there doing it. I would think there's nothing worse than for you to switch on the radio and me say, 'Hello, I'm here and I've got a very bad headache and I don't feel too good.' You'd say, 'Oh, we need all that like a hole in the head.' We all have days when we feel bad, but you get through it the best way you can. I get as much thrill out of it and enjoyment from it as I always did. The moment I found that that wasn't self-generating, I'd call it a day. If it finished tomorrow, one could never moan—it's been 35 years![16]

He was critical of the BBC's policy of banning records on the grounds of being too explicit, notably Frankie Goes to Hollywood's 'Relax', which had not been subject to the same censorship on Capital Radio. Records, he insisted, were fun—'We're talking about entertainment, aren't we?' As for anything considered suggestive, he said, 'I mean, you've really got to laugh at them.' It was 'stupid' to take them too seriously. The history of popular music, he opined, was filled with songs that clearly had much the same message. It was evident what 'I'm In The Mood For Love', recorded many times since its first appearance in the 1935 movie *Every Night at Eight*, was really about, and he said that 'it's got to be the filthiest lyric I've ever heard'. Why, he asked with amusement, did people get so uptight about what was no more than a harmless gramophone record? When the breathy '*Je T'Aime...Moi Non Plus*' by Jane Birkin and Serge Gainsbourg was banned by the BBC in 1969, he recalled that one of the newspapers had asked his opinion. He said it was the funniest record he had heard in twenty years. 'Well, can't you just see Serge Gainsbourg, who's producing the record, saying, "Jane, listen honey, can you just give us a bit more 'aaah'? All right, take 143."'[17]

After Johnny Beerling took over as Controller of Radio 1 in 1985, he decided to rest *Savile's Travels* and wanted an oldies show to replace it. The obvious choice was to bring Alan back and present the old charts on *Pick of the Pops*. He left Capital Gold (as it had become) and in January 1989 came home to the BBC to revive the *Rock Show*, with Tony Wilson as producer, and *Pick of the Pops*, produced by Phil Swern, for another few years. As he and the other presenters were aware, being a radio DJ was anything but a job for life, and he was not blind to the insecurity of it all, as he said at the time:

> I've been very comfortable over at Capital Radio and now, back at Radio 1 after all these years, I can't help wondering: is it going to work or will I fall flat on my face? But if you don't take the chance, you will never know. I would not like to go on sitting at Capital wondering what might have happened. That would niggle away at me for the rest of my days. I'm taking a chance, but it will be nice to know, one way or the other, whether I can justify whatever the brass are thinking back at Radio 1.[18]

It was an almost painfully honest statement for Alan, the most self-effacing and ridiculously modest of men. He suffered badly from depression and at one stage consulted a psychiatrist, who told Tim Blackmore that he had never before treated a patient with such low self-esteem or so little evaluation of his own worth. It was perhaps all the more surprising when the patient in question was a national broadcasting icon with a dedicated following of thousands. However, given that Alan had such a high-profile job in a notoriously precarious profession, any tendency towards feelings of insecurity would have been doubtless exacerbated. Alan once told Tim, 'If one of us had had my voice and your brains, we could have done really well'—a typically unassuming remark that summed him up perfectly. Perhaps he had problems coming to terms with just how well-known and well-loved he was by the public. His face was a familiar sight around the area where he lived, and London cabbies would happily take him from A to B without demanding payment. 'Hey, it's Fluff—pop in, mate, no charge!'

Like so many of his colleagues, Alan had always been fortunate in his unfailingly supportive producers. Tim was one, and Phil Swern was another in the latter days. Phil had first met Alan when Phil was about fifteen, when they bumped into each other at Earl's Court Station and he asked Alan for his autograph. A few years later, when he had his first job in the record industry—working on the promotion team for the Strike Records label—he went around delivering new releases to various people in the music business. When the moment came for him to take a batch over to Alan, his hero, at his home, his immediate instinct was to hand them over and run. Instead, Alan was a model of friendliness, inviting him in for a chat and later to lunch one day.

When the occasion demanded, Alan could be as flamboyant as the best of them. As with David Jacobs, Pete Murray, and the other stalwarts from the old Light Programme, in the early days, he was rarely seen not wearing a suit and tie. This gave way to more casual garb over the years. He was particularly proud of his jewellery, including a large knob of diamonds given to him by his mother, a chunky gold identity bracelet inscribed 'Fluff', and a gold wishbone ring he had bought himself. Pride of place went to an ELP enamel pendant presented to him by Manticore Records on behalf of Emerson, Lake and Palmer, as a gesture of thanks for his support, and a gold pendant that had been a fiftieth-birthday gift from two close friends, Bernie and Diana Coral of Coral's Casinos. Despite these outward trappings, he remained a remarkably modest person:

> I was always a stayer behind the barrier, and if it comes my way that's fine. I'll do my best with it, and if it doesn't on to the next, because things always kept happening like that my whole career. Things have really just come along without me being adventurous. I've never considered myself to be the kind of television person, OK? You know, I think I did the commercials all right, I think I did *Top of the Pops* all right, but I was never anything special. I don't believe I had that kind of talent. I think I've been good at putting a show together.... I think what I did BBC-wise was to just give it a little bit more excitement and a little bit of style.[19]

To several of the younger technical operators who had started working at Radio 1 in the last few years, it was a real thrill to be working with Alan—an iconic person and an iconic voice. As well as being an ultimate professional, he was always the kindest of men, not only in that he was never heard to say a bad word about anybody, but also on a personal level. He once appeared in the studio 'in a bit of a flap', needing something small but important done—probably a favour for a friend. Could anybody please help? The staff did it for him in thirty seconds flat. The following day, he was back in the studio—this time with a bottle of champagne as a thank-you.

Suddenly, the old signature tunes were back on the airwaves, but to Freeman they were effectively his private property. He was very protective of his personal cart (tape cartridge, used to play station IDs, jingles, and commercials), which was never stored in the studio but remained with him at all times. It contained a special take of 'At the Sign of the Swinging Cymbal', recorded a particular way, and he never allowed it to be copied.

Alan later explained how he maintained his enthusiasm for music:

> We're all basically lonely. The DJ is a lonely man playing to a lonely public. I'm lonely, but my loneliness is self-inflicted. I wallow in it and it's great.[20]

Looking back on the music scene at the start of the 1990s, he mused how wonderful it had been for him to be around in the business at the start of British pop and rock in the 1960s and to have seen it develop. To those who told him that 'rock today is nothing like it was,' he answered that he was very grateful. While conceding that there was more variety in the 1960s and 1970s, he stressed that if music had not changed, they would 'all be bored to death—you have to have progress'. However, he was not impressed by some of the current fare, which he found 'a little samey and bland'. While guarded in his criticism, he said he could take 'a certain amount of rap', but he found it very repetitive, while the Kylie Minogues and Jason Donovans of the world did little for him.

Around this time, a typical day at home for Alan (if not working in the studios) involved him taking the phone off the hook after lunch, spending an hour or so relaxing on his bed or in a chair, switching on some classical music and listening to it very softly until he drifted off to sleep. When he woke up, it would still be playing. Then he would go to his desk to devise ideas for a forthcoming show or work on a script. After a meal out in the evening—usually at a nearby Greek restaurant close to his home in Maida Vale—and a couple of hours in silent contemplation with a few scotch and Cokes, he would return home and turn the radio on again. He claimed that he could not think of a time when he was not listening to music of some kind—except when he was actually asleep. 'It's with me all the time,' he said. He went so far as to suggest that when the Grim Reaper called, his ideal way to go would be through a heart attack having just put 'Stairway to Heaven' on the turntable.

His peers would not have disagreed with his assessment of a DJ's life, in particular that of a single man without a partner, as Alan Freeman was to the end of his days. David Jensen considered that away from the microphone, Alan was a very quiet, even lonely man. His life revolved around his music, and his radio colleagues were his family. As a bachelor in his mid-sixties, he sometimes reflected how it might have been if he had had someone else sharing his life:

> It's very hard boomeranging off yourself all the time. And although my life is very full, there are times when I think that it would be rather nice to have had someone. I don't think one is meant to be alone in life. I would have made a good family man, but if I had kids they might have hated me still being a disc-jockey. Fortunately when you are a DJ you are in a way catering for a very large family.[21]

It was inevitable that he should sometimes question his role in a profession that until then had normally been seen as the preserve of people many years younger than him. He put it down to the fact that leading a life so involved with rock music and other DJs had 'been an inducement' not to get old, and he was a very late developer, but he was not 'ashamed' of it. If he had one unfulfilled ambition—apart from the opera singing—it was that he never did as much on television as he might have liked, but he conceded that he was better on the radio. A realist, he knew he had been very lucky. By now he could have been 'a vague memory', instead of which he had managed to remain employed for over thirty years.

Nevertheless, his lack of self-confidence still gnawed away, and he was ever keen for reassurance:

> I ask friends about how I'm doing all the time. I don't need to be told that I'm good, just that it's still working. I've always doubted myself and find that I'm increasingly saying, 'Hang about, does the pop and rock I play still connect with the public?' There must be a youthful intelligentsia who think I'm a bit of a joke doing this at 63. I understand that very well, I would be thick if I thought I connected with all young people. I'm passionately committed to my work, but I know it could end at any minute. When the BBC turn around and say, 'It's been lovely, Fluff, ta ta,' I won't be able to say I never had a chance. I don't have a great height to fall from. I've never been a star.[22]

Others who had worked at Radio 1 with him were surprised that his musical tastes remained so steadfastly consistent. Derek Chinnery went to his house one day and saw (and heard) it all for himself. 'Come on, Fluff,' he said, 'You don't really like all this heavy metal at your age?'

'I promise you I do!' Alan assured him. When Chinnery left, he could vouch for the fact that if Alan Freeman was not playing opera, it was rock music.

At the age of sixty-five, however, Alan conceded that one change had to be made; after thirty years, *Pick of the Pops* would have to come to an end, at least for the time being. Although he was reluctant to admit it, his enthusiasm for the show was waning. 'Might it not be a good idea to leave it in flight, leave it as a nice memory?' he suggested. By the end of the last show, which aired on 27 December 1992, he had long since become an institution. 'His longevity in pop proves that you did not have to die before you got old just to save face,' wrote Joe Joseph in *The Times*, marking what seemed like the end of a national institution. He acknowledged that Alan Freeman's voice had become just as recognisable as those of other media greats on the wireless, such as Alastair Cook, John Arlott, and Brian Johnston.[23] Yet his other programme still flourished, and he vowed that he would continue hosting the Saturday night rock show until he 'eventually [dropped] over that turntable and [joined] all those wondrous rockers who have gone in the sky'.

By 1993, Radio 1 was becoming obsessed with its brief to entertain the youth of the country, and new controller Matthew Bannister swept in with a mission to cull the older, more established presenters one-by-one. Hardly anyone felt or seemed to be safe. Dave Lee Travis made headlines when he resigned on air that August, telling listeners that changes were being made that went against his principles and he could not agree with them. Simon Bates, Bob Harris, Gary Davies, and others left the station shortly afterwards. Among the others was Alan Freeman, who at sixty-six was the senior Radio 1 presenter by quite a margin. Jo Whiley, who joined Radio 1 that autumn, remembered that when she was a newcomer, most of the DJs 'seemed terrified their whole world was going to collapse'. She came in one day to practise, looked across from one studio to another, and saw Alan working on the *Rock Show*. He looked over and greeted her cheerily. 'I thought, God, he knows who I am. He was the only person there who was vaguely friendly.'[24] Claire Sturgess, who had succeeded Tommy Vance on the *Friday Rock Show*, also testified to his friendliness. Far from seeing her as a threat, he was very supportive and enthusiastic about what she was doing. However, although several of the presenters and studio engineers considered that there was a strange atmosphere at Radio 1 at the time, it would be an exaggeration to call it an unfriendly place.

Bannister's brief to terminate some of the more well-established presenters on Radio 1 was thought to have been hastened, if not triggered, by TV comedians Harry Enfield and Paul Whitehouse. Their fictional characters Smashie and Nicey, who worked at 'Radio Fab FM', were parodies of several Radio 1 DJs. 'Dave Nice' (Enfield) was thought to have been based largely on Alan Freeman and Tony Blackburn, with a few elements of Tommy Vance and Dave Lee Travis as well. Alan took the joke in good heart, flattered at being sent up. He appeared in one or two Radio Fab FM sketches himself, with another new catchphrase, 'Poptastic, mate!' Nevertheless, Enfield agreed that there were two types of DJ—those who loved music, like John Peel and Alan Freeman, and those who loved the sound of their own voices.[25]

Enfield later talked to journalist Craig Brown about his first meeting with Alan. As he stood waiting outside a studio at the BBC, very loud rock music could be heard through the door. It all stopped suddenly, 'and out stumbled a nice little old man, wearing a huge pair of headphones'. Enfield also observed that Dave Lee Travis was apparently 'livid at his portrayal as Smashie', but Fluff 'seemed to relish the idea of himself as Nicey', to the extent of adding 'Poptastic!' into his collection of catchphrases.[26]

Though some of the DJs who had left the building by autumn 1993 were regarded by the media elsewhere as mere figures of fun, Alan remained a shining exception. His relentlessly upbeat manner had never masked his deep respect for the music he was playing. His colleague John Peel was never one to bestow praise if he did not mean it. During a mid-Saturday-afternoon live programme handover in the mid-1970s, John paid Alan the compliment of one of his classic tongue-in-cheek wisecracks—'I say, Alan, that pullover really goes with your hair—into the wardrobe at night.' When John was ambushed by Michael Aspel and his big red book on *This is Your Life* in December 1995 (having compered what would be his last-ever *Top of the Pops*), Alan was among the waiting guests. John told them all that in the whole history of popular music, if there was ever such a thing as a great DJ (which he disputed), Alan was it.[27] He later remarked:

> There are quite a lot of DJs who don't give away very much about themselves in the course of their programmes, Kid Jensen is another example of that. You can listen to Kid's programmes as you listen to Fluff's and really know nothing about him as a human being. I probably go the other way because I want to—sounds like showbiz muck—I want to involve the listeners in my life as much as I possibly can because I like the idea of that sense of community, but Fluff never gave away very much about himself both on the air and off, because whenever we tried to have a conversation he would go off into a lot of kind of fluffery, really. And I remember listening to Fluff, and I'm always impressed particularly when I meet people whom I genuinely admire.

As for the shows themselves, they were in a class of their own:

> They've been sort of like wedding cakes of programmes, they have been so elaborate, so ornate and highly decorated and just fantastic fun as a consequence of that and presented in such a way that you felt it was all slightly tongue-in-cheek, and Fluff certainly knew that he was going way over the top. I suppose what I'm saying really is that what he did was so easily identifiable as being him, and he did it with much brio and panache that he got away with something which would have been appalling if anyone else had been doing it.[28]

Alan did not go short of honours from his other peers either. When Tim Blackmore was asked to produce a Man of the Year presentation, he devised one to celebrate each decade in turn, with Pete Murray for the 1950s, Simon Dee for the 1960s, Johnnie Walker for the 1970s, Tony Blackburn for the 1980s, and Neil Fox of Network Chart Show fame for the 1990s. Then Alan was brought to the stage to accept his special award. Visibly moved, he said that it was a very special night for him. In the course of his acceptance speech, he told the 1,500-strong crowd that he was going to retire. They responded as one with cries of 'Oh no!' He stated that he had spoken to his manager and he had decided that he was going to retire—in the year 2020.

Nobody would have minded if Fluff had been another Alan Keith, still presenting into his nineties. At almost seventy years of age, however, he was increasingly a martyr to chronic asthma and arthritis. The latter gradually spread from the base of his spine to his legs, and it was so severe that sometimes he could hardly stand. Deafness was also getting the better of him. He could no longer drink alcohol, and he missed his glass of white wine.

Nevertheless, in his twilight years it seemed as if there was hardly a radio station in Britain that was not eager to employ him. On Capital Gold, he hosted *Pick of the Pops Take Three* from April 1994 until January 1997. This overlapped to an extent with *The Friday Rock Show* on Virgin Radio, while he also was presenting one-off shows on Classic FM at around the same time, sometimes as a stand-in for Paul Gambaccini. Alan also appeared on a short programme in the Radio 4 series *Kaleidoscope* in August 1997, in which he looked back on more than forty years of broadcasting—first in Australia and then in England, hopping from one station to another with the BBC and independent radio, and, as often as not, hopping back again. By no means stuck in the past, he also mused on some of the more recent artists who particularly impressed him, among them Marti Pellow of Wet Wet Wet, Celine Dion,

Ronan Keating, and Gary Barlow, the possessor of 'a better voice than most people give him credit for'.

It was only fitting that Alan's career should come full circle; as far as British listeners were concerned, it came to a graceful end more or less where it began. In 1997, *Pick of the Pops*, featuring the Top 20 from two separate years, came home to Radio 2. Phil Swern, who had been a producer for Alan since his days at Capital Radio, was responsible for noting the timings of each track in the running order. Sometimes he found Alan a little inattentive, and to wake him up he had to poke him gently with a stick. This worked perfectly well until one day, when Johnny Beerling was showing some VIPs around the studio and was horrified to see one of the elder statesmen of BBC music broadcasting apparently being physically attacked.

That same year, Alan also began to present a classical and opera show on the same station, *Their Greatest Bits*. This was the brainchild of Tim Blackmore, who had co-founded the Unique Production Company in 1983, with Neil Myners as producer. They had initially had mixed feelings about the title of *Their Greatest Bits*, feeling it might be rather disrespectful to the classics, but they need not have worried. Radio 2 Controller Jim Moir, a staunch champion of Alan and his presence on the station, loved the idea and title and knew they had a potential winner. Alan justified everyone's faith and relished presenting it as much as his listeners enjoyed tuning in. The show resulted in another compilation album, *Alan Freeman's Classical Bits*, which featured twenty-three tracks on a double CD. Another well-deserved accolade came in 1998, when his years of service to broadcasting were recognised by the award of an MBE and an investiture at Buckingham Palace.

For as long as he was physically able, Alan enjoyed something of a broadcaster's Indian summer as he continued to do what he loved best. He was chauffeur-driven to the BBC studios in order to pre-record his shows for Radio 2, which retained his distinctive character. One off-the-cuff link was particularly well-remembered by colleagues and listeners; after playing The Ivy League's 'Tossing and Turning', he asked the audience, 'Well—are you a tosser or a turner?'

By 1999, however, Alan had to use a walking frame, and that December he was admitted to hospital. Doctors suspected he had suffered a minor stroke, although tests remained inconclusive. Early the following year, he had two falls at his flat in west London, and on doctor's orders he went to live at Brinsworth House in Twickenham, a retirement home for actors and performers run by the Entertainment Artistes' Benevolent Fund. As a resident, he was much-loved in his new surroundings and invariably the life and soul of the party. Perhaps it only takes a small leap of imagination to picture him seated at the home, behind a couple of record decks and a microphone, with his headphones on and jingles at the ready, providing the entertainment for fellow residents on vinyl or CD.

Alan presented his last *Pick of the Pops* in April 2000, then handing over the reins to Dale Winton. It had become an effort, as he said, because he 'didn't quite have the bite [he] used to, and if you're frightened of doing something then it's probably a good idea to pack it in'.[29] One month later, he was presented with the Lifetime Achievement Award at the Sony Radio Academy Awards. He was given a standing ovation at the ceremony, as Dale Winton saluted 'a man who has served and is held in the highest affection by every sector of our industry'. *Pick of the Pops* would live on as a staple feature on Radio 2, with Dale in the chair until October 2010 and Tony Blackburn for the next few years.

On 29 December 2001, Radio 2 listeners were presented with an affectionate tribute, *The Complete Fluff ... Not 'Alf!* With recollections from the man himself and several colleagues, as well as tributes from Sir Paul McCartney and Ian Gillan, it was presented by Noel Edmonds, who opined in his introduction that 'he legitimised that verbal crutch of the inarticulate', sidestepping the fact that all the apparent hesitations were done purely for effect, carefully scripted in advance, and that Alan was an extremely articulate man. Paul Gambaccini also put his finger on his colleague's success, arguing that Alan had 'retained complete credibility by sending himself up' and not taking himself too seriously. Journalist Craig Brown observed:

> ... like the 1 and the 0 in the binary system, he would rearrange these catch-phrases from sentence to sentence and somehow each new combination would add up to something different.[30]

Alan continued to record *Their Greatest Bits* prior to transmission until March 2003, but when he developed osteomyelitis in the jaw, he was forced to give up the unequal struggle. One month later, he was inducted into the Radio Academy Hall of Fame.

Once retired, Alan's final years were overshadowed by his increasing ill health. He made his last public appearance at Golders Green Crematorium in March 2005, attending the funeral of his friend and erstwhile colleague Tommy Vance. As he sat in a wheelchair, pushed around by another former Radio 1 DJ, Simon Bates, a line of about thirty people who had not seen him for years were queueing up to shake him by the hand. He was visibly bemused and touched by it all. Maybe they sensed that it was not just a farewell to the man whose memory they had come to honour, but also to Alan Freeman himself.

In the autumn of 2006, he was admitted to West Middlesex Hospital with a chest infection; he died on 27 November, aged seventy-nine. His funeral took place on 7 December at South West Middlesex Crematorium, and it was attended by several of his former colleagues, including Paul Gambaccini, Dave Lee Travis, Simon Bates, and Nicky Campbell.

Among the tributes paid to him was a heartfelt one from Tim Blackmore, the man who had been associated with him on a professional basis for longer than anybody else. He observed that Freeman, with his passion for music of all kinds and his longevity as a presenter:

> ... retained a total bewilderment that so much success and affection should have come his way. His was the creation of the chart countdown, his was the stunning combination of rock music and classical music, and his was the creation of minimalism in the art of the DJ.[31]

In 2009, Robin Gibb, destined to fall victim to cancer only three years later, wrote and released his own tribute, 'Alan Freeman Days'. Like his brothers, the Bee Gees vocalist had made the passage from Australia to Britain many years earlier, and he had always been grateful to Alan for his tireless support of the group in their pursuit of global recognition, as well as his championship of Gibb's initial solo material. Now, his song mentioned the passing of John Lennon, Marc Bolan, his twin brother Maurice, and the pain inside, 'the day that Alan Freeman died'.

3
John Peel

Over a four-decade career, John Peel reinvented himself time and time again. Outside the studio, he was quiet and self-effacing, yet on air he could be outspoken, opinionated, and often trod where no other presenter would go. He may sometimes have exasperated his bosses and listeners, but he never forfeited their admiration or respect. According to friend and long-time Radio 1 producer John Walters, he was arguably the single most important individual in the history of British rock music.[1]

John Robert Parker Ravenscroft was born in Heswall Cottage Hospital, near Liverpool, on 30 August 1939. A solitary youngster, he loved listening to Radio Luxembourg and the American Forces Network, and it was always an ambition to host his own radio programme so he could play the music he wanted to hear and share with others. As a boarder at Shrewsbury School, he found an understanding mentor in his housemaster, R. H. J. Brooke, who wrote perceptively on one of his school reports:

> Perhaps it's possible that John can form some kind of nightmarish career out of his enthusiasm for unlistenable records and his delight in writing long and facetious essays.[2]

'Brookie' was more supportive of the unconventional lad than this report might suggest. Years later, John confessed his gratitude to the man who recognised that academically he was hopeless, but tried to channel his natural instincts into something more productive; John later remembered, 'He rather liked the idea of having a disruptive influence in his house.'[3] When John's children became newspaper crossword addicts (like him), he felt he owed some of his skills to a public school education. One afternoon he was shopping in Oxford Street when his mobile phone rang. It was his daughter Flossie. 'Writing desk, ten letters?' she asked.

'Escritoire,' he replied at once.[4]

His required reading each week in the 1950s included *New Musical Express*, in which he read for the first time about the charismatic new singing sensation across the Atlantic, Elvis Presley. The Light Programme of those days was quite a staid institution, so it was a red-letter day for many when *Two-Way Family Favourites*, a family request slot hosted by the husband-and-wife team Cliff Michelmore and Jean Metcalfe, played 'Heartbreak Hotel'. For John, it was a moment he never forgot.

After school, he had a stint in national service as a radar operator in the Royal Artillery and then took a job at Townhead Mill in Rochdale. In 1960 he went to America as a travelling insurance salesman for a cotton producer who had business connections with his father, and then as a computer programmer. After President Kennedy was assassinated in November 1963, John passed himself off as a reporter for the *Liverpool Echo* so he could attend the arraignment of Lee Harvey Oswald. Beatlemania would sweep America within a few weeks, as it had already done in England. Partly on the strength of a fictitious association with the Fab Four, and partly though his Merseyside origins, he bluffed himself into his first radio job, unpaid, working for WRR (AM) in Dallas, presenting the second hour of *Kat's Karavan*, a show on Monday nights. Similar stints followed for KOMA in Oklahoma City and for KMEN in San Bernardino, where he worked as John Ravencroft (minus the 's'). While there, in 1965, he married Shirley Anne Milburn. Only later did he discover that she and her family had lied about her age and that she was only fifteen, eleven years younger than him.

Also while working for KMEN he went to see a live group, The Misunderstood. A blues-based outfit who were among the first to experiment with guitar feedback, they impressed him so much that he later saw it as 'like one of your St Paul on the road to Damascus experiences'.[5] He financed an album's worth of recorded material with them and suggested they try their luck in London. They secured a record deal there, thanks partly to some contacts of John's younger brother, Alan, and released a single, 'I Can Take You To The Sun', at the end of 1966. After the lead vocalist, Rick Brown, was drafted into the Army, the group never managed to capitalise on what had seemed a promising start.

John also returned to England, now out of work and in a 'fairly catastrophic marriage', living with his semi-estranged wife and his mother in Notting Hill. Their future prospects did not seem too bright. Fortunately, a neighbour had connections with Alan Keen, the programme controller of Radio London, one of the main offshore pirate radio stations, affectionately known among its DJs and supporters as 'Big L'. John did not have to audition as the staff at the London offices in Curzon Street were impressed with his experience as a presenter in California. With his unhappy domestic life, the idea of being on a ship two weeks out of three was a very inviting one. At the suggestion of a Radio London secretary, he adopted the name 'John Peel'. He presented a daytime show, 'just the regular Radio London fare' of mainly new releases and current chart singles, and a show from midnight to 2.00 a.m. that was initially called *London after Midnight*. Radio London was a tightly formatted Top 40 station, but this particular show was allowed some flexibility over what music was played, tending to reflect the taste of whoever was hosting it. When John joined the station he continued this tradition, but his taste was somewhat different to that of his colleagues. After a while, the programme formally became known as *The Perfumed Garden*.

At first, he presented the show in a similar style to his daytime slot, with commercials, weather, news, 'and all of the things that [he] was supposed to do'. Soon it dawned on him that nobody in the Radio London office— let alone the people on the ship—seemed to be listening to him at night. He began to improvise; he gradually stopped running the ads and so on in order to play more of the mainly psychedelic music of Captain Beefheart and his Magic Band, Jefferson Airplane, and others, which he had brought back from America with him. To this he added a British dimension, with album tracks from Jimi Hendrix, The Incredible String Band, and Pink Floyd, among others. The new format attracted plenty of eager listeners, who sent him letters and poetry, much of which he read out on air. In between records, he also discussed current issues such as The Rolling Stones' recent drug charges. Alan Keen was unaware of the show's content until Brian Epstein, the Beatles' manager, wrote to congratulate him on having such an enterprising programme in his schedule. A curious Keen listened in and was horrified by the content, but as Radio London's days were numbered, he felt there was nothing he could do about it.

During the final weeks of pirate radio broadcasting, John was receiving far more mail than his colleagues. The station closed on 14 August 1967; for two years afterwards, until summer 1969, he wrote a column under the title 'The Perfumed Garden' for the underground newspaper *International Times*. The column demonstrated his credentials as a supporter (if not always an uncritical one) of the ideals of the underground. As far as drugs were concerned, he had smoked grass in California but did not care for the taste of home-grown joints once he returned to Britain. He dropped acid twice in his life, but he said he found it was like visiting Stratford-upon-Avon—having already done it, he did not feel the need to do so again.[6]

Like the other Radio London pirate DJs, he was not unemployed for long; he too found a place on BBC 'Wonderful Radio 1', which began broadcasting on 30 September. He was one of the first to join the station, aided by the fact that the Radio 1 hierarchy seemed to have no real idea what they were doing and had to take on people from the pirate ships because there was no one else available. His initial letter and sample tape was sent to Mark White, Deputy Head of the BBC Gramophone

Department, and he received a polite acknowledgement in return. It took a little help from Clive Selwood, of Elektra Records, and Bernie Andrews, one of the more forward-looking radio producers, to push the door open wider.

At the beginning of its existence, Radio 1 was allowed more needle time than the Light Programme, which it replaced, but the days of standalone broadcasting around the clock were some way ahead. It combined some of its programming with Radio 2, which was pitched at an older listenership. John began broadcasting on 1 October 1967 on *Top Gear*, which aired from 2.00 to 5.00 p.m. on Sunday afternoons, presenting jointly with Pete Drummond. Both shared duties with other DJs at first, including Mike Ahern (a former Radio Caroline DJ who lasted one show on Radio 1 and then went to work in Australia), Rick Dane (who was gone within a few months), and Tommy Vance.

The forty-six DJs hired to launch Radio 1 were given eight-week contracts on the understanding that several would be weeded out fairly soon. At the time, no one, least of all John himself, thought he would stay there for long. The presenters were pictured in a mostly smiling group shot on the steps of All Souls Church, Langham Place, the offices of Radio 1. Included in the photo were Tony Blackburn, Jimmy Young, and Terry Wogan, who were seen as reliable, safe pairs of hands, guaranteed to toe the line come hell or high water. Few would have given John—sitting in the bottom corner, his unsmiling face looking away from the camera—much of a chance. Even fewer would have thought that he would literally have a job on Radio 1 for the rest of his life—in his case, thirty-seven years. The founding Station Controller, Robin Scott, admitted 'there was a feeling in-house that John was almost too much his own man to let loose'.[7] Looking back, thirty years later, John said there was a kind of healthy paranoia about Radio 1 at the beginning, which kept them all on their toes. They assumed that it would not last very long, and that 'even if Radio 1 continued, [the DJs] would very likely not.'[8] He owed his survival largely to having two ever-supportive producers, firstly Bernie Andrews and then John Walters, a former musician who had played the trumpet in The Alan Price Set. Working with John Peel, he said, was like taking a dog for a walk—'You just have to make sure he doesn't cock his leg at any musical lamp-post for too long.'[9]

In his early days, John met with one of the senior Radio 1 staff members. He was unimpressed with the physical appearance of his employee, who sported a kaftan and hair down to his shoulders. Nevertheless, conversation ensued, and John referred to public school. The senior gentleman asked if John knew anybody who had attended one.

'Went to one myself, actually,' Peel informed him. 'Shrewsbury, Riggs Hall.'

'How's old Brookie?' the man enquired, suggesting that John had suddenly gone up in his estimation. With that, Peel knew that his contract was safe for at least another three months.[10]

Top Gear immediately became renowned as a programme that was put together by its presenters and producers with care. Instead of relying on a diet of current hits and oldies, it featured specially recorded sessions and album tracks from what generally went under the blanket name of 'underground music', including The Jimi Hendrix Experience (ironically a group who had scored four Top 20 hits in Britain that year), Jefferson Airplane, the Grateful Dead, Soft Machine, and Leonard Cohen. One session on the first show was provided by The Move, whose hit single at the time, 'Flowers in the Rain', had been the first record played in full on the station. Other sessions for that show featured Traffic (also briefly Top 10 regulars), Tomorrow, Pink Floyd, and Tim Rose. Bernie Andrews had suggested that *Top Gear* should be a double-headed show with a professional anchorman and another guest DJ each week.

John Peel and Tommy Vance were established as the joint presenters of the show from 12 November 1967. Thanks largely to the championship of Bernie Andrews, John was given solo charge of *Top Gear* from 4 February 1968, remaining at the helm until it came to an end in September 1975. He was proud to be immortalised in the 'Pseuds' Corner' section of *Private Eye* as the man who wrote that the music of Pink Floyd evoked the sound of dying galaxies, although he was sure he had pinched the line from another source.[11] In 1969, the BBC issued a compilation album, *John Peel Presents Top Gear*, consisting mainly of tracks from Ron Geesin, Bridget St John, Sweet Marriage, and The BBC Radiophonic Workshop's experiments with John's voice itself.

Meanwhile, John presented an additional show, *Night Ride*, which began in March 1968 and lasted for eighteen months. This was an extension of *The Perfumed Garden*, where he was given more or less *carte blanche* to cater for an older audience. Advertised by the BBC as 'an exploration of words and music', it featured rock, folk, blues, classical, electronic, and non-Western music (later known as world music) from the BBC Sound Archive, as well as poetry readings and interviews with guests, including Marc Bolan (at that time singer and guitarist with the acoustic duo Tyrannosaurus Rex), musician and journalist Mick Farren, and Bridget St John. Renowned for its rather anti-establishment stance, the show was something of a thorn in the side for the BBC top brass, who saw it nervously as a token programme for 'the underground' and a sop to the radical youth of the day—for whom they were catering through gritted teeth.

As the presenter, John often lived dangerously, working a little outside the rules, going where other DJs did not dare to tread, and in doing so becoming notoriously practiced in the art of survival against the odds. One particularly controversial show was in November 1968, when a guest, the satirist John Wells, criticised Prime Minister Harold Wilson for his apparent indifference to starvation caused by the civil war in Nigeria. Rarely one to take criticism in the media lightly, Wilson demanded an apology, which John Peel was obliged to read out on the next show. The following month, John Lennon and Yoko Ono were invited on partly to promote their forthcoming album, *Two Virgins*, an avant-garde release and probably Lennon's worst-selling record ever. Complaints were made that material on the show that night was 'suggestive', but annoyed listeners should have been grateful that it was not television and they were therefore spared a view of the record's notorious cover and its full-frontal nudity.

Six months later, John was in trouble again after hosting a trailer for another BBC programme on venereal disease, and said casually on air that he had recently suffered from a sexually transmitted disease. There were demands in the press that he should be dismissed. Fervent apologies, and the stout defence of his producers, ensured that he lived to fight another day—or in his case, another three decades and more. One or two other Radio 1 DJs of the age, notoriously the similarly maverick Kenny Everett, sailed a little too close to the wind and never led quite the same charmed life.

John could always be guaranteed to speak his mind. Interviewed by a student paper in 1967, he had made his contempt plain for *Top of the Pops*. To him it was 'a national disgrace', reflecting the very worst in popular taste, with no attempt being made to present anything remotely progressive or innovative. 'Anyone who appears on the thing,' he concluded, 'should be ashamed of themselves.'[12] Ironically, he was invited onto the show one week in early 1968 as a guest co-presenter with Jimmy Savile. He was supposed to introduce Amen Corner, but either nerves or forgetfulness got the better of him. 'And next... er...' A furious Savile told him afterwards that he would ensure Peel never appeared on television again.

Some of the top brass at Radio 1 were likewise unenthusiastic about his presence on Radio 1. When *Melody Maker* published its Readers' Poll in September 1968, John was voted 'Top DJ' and *Top Gear* was voted 'Top Radio Show'; the Radio 1 management was astonished that Tony Blackburn had not won. The paper said the awards proved that the show was not a minority-appeal programme any more. Many listeners evidently did want sessions from the likes of Yes, The Strawbs, Ten Years After, and Caravan after all, and they were not satisfied with a mere diet of the Top 40.

For the first nine years or so of his life at Radio 1, John's eclectic tastes enabled him to embrace the mainstream as well as what was labelled the underground or the progressive music scene. As a reviewer of new singles for two of the weekly music papers—firstly *Disc and Music Echo* and then *Sounds*—he was opinionated but also quite accommodating at the same time, acknowledging chart-orientated acts who had nevertheless demonstrated some imagination in their work. For example, The Marmalade had striven for artistic credibility and control over what they recorded after being turned into a hit factory, recording other people's songs, by their previous label. John gave them heartfelt praise for their 1971 Top 10 single 'Cousin Norman'. Elvis Presley, who was reduced to churning out mainly lacklustre ballads that sold largely on the strength of his name, would regularly receive a critical mauling from John, who knew he could make much better records and were frustrated by his failure to do so. He also evinced underwhelming enthusiasm for offerings by the Osmonds, both their group recordings and their individual solo records. When asked to choose his least favourite single of 1972, he said he seldom heard anything that was totally without redemption, but 'Long Haired Lover from Liverpool' by Little Jimmy Osmond came as close as any.[13]

One group that he was proud to champion at the time was The Faces. He later recalled when he first met the members:

> [I thought they were] impossibly rowdy and vulgar people and then it occurred to me that possibly they were having a much better time than I was. I liked the noise they made and their attitude to it.[14]

Records by The Faces and their frontman, Rod Stewart, received generous airplay on John's programme. Stewart was simultaneously contracted to record solo albums—with assistance from members of the group and additional musicians—for a different label. When his 'Maggie May' was released as a single and he and The Faces were invited to promote it on *Top of the Pops*, they wanted John to join them and mime the mandolin part on the record (played by Ray Jackson of Lindisfarne) as a thank-you for his support. A Musicians' Union official reluctantly agreed to the request on the condition that John did not pluck the instrument or make any serious attempt to play it. Being sympathetic to trade unions, he readily agreed, and was relieved when he sensed the cameraman was trying to keep him out of shot most of the time. He needn't have worried; a shy man sitting on a stool, pretending to mime, was hardly likely to steal attention away from the microphone-stand-twirling vocalist and his associates, who ended up their equally mimed performance (albeit with live vocal) by kicking a football around the studio.

Having got regularly drunk on bourbon while in America, John had returned to England determined to clean himself up. Thanks to his girlfriend, Sheila Gilhooly (soon to become the second Mrs Ravenscroft), John Walters (who had succeeded Bernie Andrews as Peel's producer), and to nights out with The Faces, he got back into drinking again—not to excess, but enough to enjoy convivial nights on the town.[15] The group invited him to join them on their tour towards the end of 1972; by the time of their date in Blackpool that December, he had become overwhelmed by the group's acceptance of him and the sense of occasion. Backstage, he noted afterwards, he had 'that feeling that comes only when a band is really hitting it right, when it seems as though some unseen hand is reaching right down inside you and dragging out all the hang-ups and inhibitions in there and flinging them away'. Their music had him 'dancing quietly in the corner of the backstage area with tears streaming down [his] cheeks and an idiot grin on [his] face'.[16] By his own admission, he was never the world's most animated dancer, but he did devise his own personalised boogie, 'a kind of energetic, springy, shuffling walk on the spot'. His family christened the dance 'Westbourne Grove Walk', as the first sighting they had of it was when he returned from Westbourne Grove and started performing it as he told his wife what he had been doing that day.[17]

He was less fortunate with another performer whose initial success he had helped to nurture. Marc Bolan and Tyrannosaurus Rex had enjoyed a small but devoted following, with John supporting them, writing a sleeve note for one of their albums, reading a story on another, and broadcasting several sessions from them on his show. When they expanded, went electric, and became T. Rex in 1970, Peel was as glad as anyone when their second single under this reincarnation, 'Hot Love', topped the charts for six weeks in 1971. However, when he was less than impressed with the almost equally successful follow-up 'Get It On', Marc dropped him as a friend and refused to take or return his phone calls. On his final *Top Gear* programme in September 1975—a retrospective of major acts featured over the years—he included two songs from the duo 'as they were changing from Tyrannosaurus Rex to T. Rex', which, in his view, had not been an entirely happy move, but had 'done fairly well for them'; he thus managed to avoid mentioning Bolan by name. When Marc was killed in a car accident two years later, John paid tribute in his *Sounds* column to a man who had 'made the transition from bopping elf and hero of the flower-folk to fully fledged teen idol and *TOTP* staple', and had thus gone from his life. John said, 'I was sad then, as I am now, to see him go.'[18]

Notwithstanding his criticism of T. Rex's later material, he gave several of their glam-rock contemporaries a fair hearing in his capacity as a music press reviewer. Despite disgruntled comments from some readers, he would put in a good word for singles by Sweet and Gary

Glitter, long before the latter's chequered career ended in irredeemable disgrace. Peel also wrote that a new single by Slade in June 1973, the endearingly raucous 'Skweeze Me, Pleeze Me', had 'enriched our drab miserable lives'. Easy-listening pop like Dawn's 'Tie a Yellow Ribbon Round the Old Oak Tree' and The Carpenters' 'Jambalaya' could expect an equally honest but rather more brutal verdict.

By this point, *Top Gear* was by and large considered to be a fairly serious programme. However, another performer who, like Rod Stewart, had made the transition to global superstardom could also be relied on from time to time to bring an element of fun to the proceedings. In December 1973, Elton John—rarely out of the Top 10 at the time—recorded a festive session for John's Christmas Day show. John Walters got a crate of light ales in, they hired an upright pub piano, invited several Radio 1 producers and other staff along to create an atmosphere, and the performer regaled them with a medley of Christmas tunes. When Walters suggested he do something else in pub-piano style, he played a Bob Dylan medley, old standards like 'Down at the Old Bull and Bush', and then what he called a 'kamikaze act' of his own hits 'Daniel' and 'Your Song' on the basis that if anybody was going to have a good time destroying his own work, it might as well be him. As he played and sang, everybody else present clinked their beer bottles, sang along, and Walters could be heard calling out 'Last orders!'[19]

John Peel observed that even the very best of rock music at that time was 'essentially ephemeral'. It had been around for less than twenty years, and pundits of the 1950s had proclaimed that Elvis Presley, Eddie Cochran, Fats Domino, and the other pioneer rock 'n' rollers would not last; instead, they argued, the enduring music of that era would be the 'jazz and serious pop'. Who, John asked, could name any exponents of the latter? Everyone knew the greatest hits of Elvis, Eddie, and Fats. Pundits in 1973 might be claiming that Yes and Emerson, Lake and Palmer would be the ones most fondly remembered, but John contended that they would have largely vanished from memory, with Sweet and Gary Glitter seen as representing the true sound of the '70s. Whenever he was told that a record by a contemporary rock musician was a work of lasting interest, his natural reaction was to reach for his hat and head for the wide-open spaces.

To every rule there was an exception, and he had just come across a record 'of such strength, energy and real beauty that to [him] it [represented] the first breakthrough into history that any musician [had] made'.[20] The record that had earned his unqualified praise was Mike Oldfield's 'Tubular Bells', a largely instrumental epic that had been rejected by several established record companies. It appeared as the first release on the new Virgin label, and for some years it was rarely far from the album chart. This was one occasion on which he and many critics were at one with each other. It was not the case a couple of years later, in November 1975, when he saw Bruce Springsteen live at the Hammersmith Odeon. He opined that the first few numbers by Springsteen (who was being hailed by *Rolling Stone* as the future of rock 'n' roll) 'were a trifle theatrical, like off-cuts from *West Side Story*', and 'he rather overdid the street punk routine'.[21]

Springsteen had been hailed by some as 'the new Bob Dylan', but John was always glad to play records by the old Dylan on his show, sometimes before anybody else in Britain. In the first week of January 1976, he heard that Capital Radio was claiming it had an exclusive on the new Dylan album, *Desire*, on the show hosted by Nicky Horne, the commercial station's equivalent to John Peel. Keen to beat them at their own game, one of John's staff telephoned CBS Records to check; to his delight, John learned that the company had a pre-release white label copy available, and they would immediately send it to him at the BBC. He could hardly believe his luck. That night, he started his programme by saying how annoying it was that another station would have an exclusive of the album the following evening; he proceeded to play it from start to finish himself. The next morning, he was amused to hear Capital Radio still telling listeners that Horne would have the first play of the record that evening. To deflate them further, he passed his advance copy to Johnnie Walker so he could feature a track or two on his lunchtime show.[22]

At the beginning of the decade, John had had his own 'catastrophically unsuccessful' record label, Dandelion, named after his pet hamster. Launched in the summer of 1969 with the aid of Clive Selwood, Peel's initial purpose had been to have his own outlet so he could release an album by Bridget St John, and he produced her debut, *Ask Me No Questions*. During its three-year history, Dandelion released twenty-seven albums by eighteen different artists, plus a handful of singles, and a sampler album, *There Is Some Fun Going Forward*, the sleeve of which portrayed a discreetly naked Mr Peel in the bath with a female companion. Among the other acts on their books were Stackwaddy—a punk group long before their time, who, in John's words, 'played a rather violent and inaccurate R&B'—and the extravagantly named Principal Edwards Magic Theatre.[23] Another of their acts was comedian Bill Oddie, who made a one-off single produced by John, 'On Ilkla Moor Baht'At', performed as a parody of Joe Cocker's 'With a Little Help From My Friends'. The keyboards on the record were the work of Verden Allen from Mott The Hoople; John recalled that Verden kept on playing the notes the wrong way round, but they wearied of him getting it wrong after several takes and kept the recording as it was.

Only one Dandelion release, Medicine Head's single '(And The) Pictures In The Sky', ever made the British chart, becoming a Top 30 hit in 1971. John admitted that the project was never a financial success, losing money on every record released bar one, but he had enjoyed having a label as it was good to be able 'to put out stuff that [he] liked without, in those days, having to worry about whether it was going to work commercially'. Dandelion folded in 1972, and John had the dubious pleasure of seeing its two brightest hopes, Medicine Head and Clifford T. Ward, being rewarded with Top 10 singles after signing to other labels the following year.

John had a brief role in one episode of *The Goodies*, continuing his connection with Bill Oddie. Shown in July 1973, the episode featured Oddie as pop star 'Randy Pandy', appearing on *Top of the Pops* and being introduced by John, who wore a blonde wig and impersonated Jimmy Savile. Ironically, he later called *The Goodies* one of the least amusing comedy shows ever witnessed by mankind and also gave their most successful single, 'Do The Funky Gibbon', a thumbs-down review in *Sounds*. About twenty years later, he said that the trio, or rather two of them, tried to beat him up one evening in the Marquee Club in London, and he was rescued by Robert Plant. He added dryly that he would not have minded if it had been someone fashionable. One of the Goodies, Graeme Garden, said this was the most ludicrous piece of gossip he had ever heard.

John's marriage to Shirley Anne Milburn had proved increasingly acrimonious. Soon after they settled in England, the differences between them became irreconcilable; they divorced in 1973 and she returned to America, where she eventually took her own life. In later years, he avoided talking about her altogether, and when faced by one particularly persistent press interviewer, the result was 'an unusual and difficult silence.'[24] In November 1968, while they were separated, he met Sheila Gilhooly, a teaching student whom he affectionately referred to on air and in his various newspaper columns as 'The Pig', as she apparently had a tendency to snort whenever she laughed. They married in August 1974; it was to be an extremely happy lifelong union.

John was the last of the Radio 1 presenters who could be imagined hosting a roadshow or anything similar. He took pride in having only seen one such event in his life—when he travelled to Brighton to review it for the *Observer*. However, he was eventually asked to take part in a Radio 1 'fun day'—what he called his version of 'DJ hell'. In May 1975, a Brands Hatch race meeting was held at Mallory Park in the East Midlands, with nearly all the DJs present alongside special guests The Bay City Rollers, then at the peak of their popularity, and The Three Degrees. The event was oversubscribed, with about 47,000 people present. It ended in chaos when the Rollers were taken out by helicopter to an island on a lake in the middle of the grounds. Hordes of desperate fans, longing to get as close to their idols as possible, tried to wade through the lake and had to be forcibly moved back to safety. Meanwhile, a speedboat piloted by a Womble (alias Mike Batt) was driving around on the water with Tony Blackburn on board, waving cheerily to the crowds while they tried desperately not to hit anyone. As John always loved telling people, he was astonished by the apparent surrealism of such an event, telling fellow presenter Johnnie Walker to look on it and marvel, as they would never see anything like it again.[25]

Until the mid-1970s, John's tastes and the records he played on his programme were by and large an eclectic mix. In July 1974, he wrote in his weekly column for *Sounds* that his shows were roughly based on the principle that whatever his listeners were buying, listening to and enjoying was all very well, 'but there exists also something else, less favoured, but equally worthy of your attention'. The previous night's *Top Gear* had featured a remarkable variety of records by Sandy Denny, Don Covay, Cream, Sweet, Ry Cooder, the Fatback Band, Eric Clapton, Joni Mitchell, and Sunny Ade and His African Beats.[26] His fifteen favourite singles of 1975 encompassed the No. 1 hits 'I'm Not In Love' by 10cc, Rod Stewart's 'Sailing', the traditional folk-rock of Jack the Lad's 'Gentleman Soldier', reggae sensation Bob Marley and the Wailers' 'No Woman No Cry', the belated British single release of John Lennon's 'Imagine', and, at No. 1, Bebop Deluxe's 'Maid in Heaven'. Perhaps the most remarkable inclusion in the list was 'The Trail of the Lonesome Pine' from the soundtrack of the Laurel and Hardy movie *Way Out West*. The United Artists label had issued an album of clips from the comedy duo's pictures and put the song out on 45 rpm, more as a promotional device than in the hope of chart success. Record company staff were astonished when John featured it one night, regretting that it was nobody on Radio 1's record of the week, 'but it could easily be [his]'. Once his daytime colleagues began airing it, the momentum was unstoppable, and only Queen's 'Bohemian Rhapsody' prevented it from topping the chart that December.

No one could have foreseen that within twelve months, John's approach would change dramatically. His new show would bear no relation to the old one apart from the man behind the microphone. When John heard a new album by the Ramones in 1976, the effect on him was similar to when he had first heard Little Richard. He played several tracks on his show, and disgruntled listeners made their views plain. Within weeks, he had acquired many listeners who were thrilled that somebody was playing punk rock on the radio. Nevertheless, that summer, those who had tuned in for several years could expect to hear not only Eddie and the Hot Rods, Jonathan Richman and the Modern Lovers, and The 101ers, but also sessions from Shanghai, Lone Star, and AC/DC, plus regular plays of new singles by Dave Edmunds and Nick Lowe and Eric Clapton's new album, *No Reason to Cry*, in full.

Records by The Saints and The Damned (and a session by the latter) would follow on the show towards the end of the year. In December, the Sex Pistols made the front pages of the tabloid press by swearing live on teatime television, dealing a mortal blow to the career of their interviewer, Bill Grundy. Radio 1 Station Controller Derek Chinnery asked producer John Walters to confirm that Radio 1 was not 'getting behind this filth', or, in other words, not playing any of this dreadful punk rock that was being written about in the papers. Walters must have been amused to inform Chinnery that John had played little else for the last few days, and that The Damned had been in the BBC studios for a session.[27] The Sex Pistols' first single, 'Anarchy in the UK', had been released in November, and it was excluded from daytime airplay on Radio 1. John played it anyway, and the record stayed in the Top 40 for three weeks before EMI withdrew it from sale and terminated the group's contact. The group were never invited to record a session for the show. Walters, a former art teacher, had gone to see them, with The Clash as support, at The 100 Club in Oxford Street in August. He was tempted to book them, but having seen 'all the spitting and banging' and having looked into Johnny Rotten's eyes, he decided that he would not like to be in the studio with them or inflict them on anybody else. Rotten was not the kind of man anyone would trust to give out the scissors.[28]

In December 1976, John invited listeners to name their all-time favourite tracks, a practice that (with variations) would become an annual tradition. The first such chart, just too early to feature any punk rock, was an interesting mix of rock and progressive rock from the previous ten years. Bob Dylan and Pink Floyd both featured twice in the top ten, with Jimi Hendrix, the Beatles, and Led Zeppelin featuring twice in the top twenty; the latter topped the poll with 'Stairway to Heaven'.

John's programme underwent a transitional phase during 1977. Within a few months, he had gained thousands of younger listeners to replace the older element; in his words, 'all those people who wanted to go on listening to Grateful Dead records for the rest of their lives obviously got off the train at that point'.[29] As his show went out late at night, he was the only BBC presenter allowed to play the Sex Pistols' 'God Save The Queen', a single released after they had been signed by and dropped from two major record labels in quick succession due to their unseemly behaviour and then signed by the less easily shockable Virgin label. The record was banned from daytime radio and *Top of the Pops*, and most high-street record shops refused to stock it. Records by The Stranglers, the Buzzcocks, Graham Parker and

The Rumour, and others were played regularly, but John seemed concerned not to alienate his older listenership too quickly. Sessions were still recorded featuring what he and Walters called 'straight' acts, including Thin Lizzy, The Boys of the Lough, June Tabor, Medicine Head, and John Martyn. Thin Lizzy occupied a unique position; although they had been part of the hard rock mainstream, their attitude, personality, and their readiness to embrace the punk rock ethos meant they could hardly be consigned to the dinosaur brigade. They even collaborated live with two members of the Sex Pistols, performing as 'The Greedy Bastards'—although the name was abbreviated to 'The Greedies' when they joined forces for a one-off Christmas 1979 hit single, 'A Merry Jingle'.

New singles and tracks from albums by Fleetwood Mac and The Eagles were still featured on the show, although he seemed anxious not to show too much enthusiasm when he played them. At the end of the year, he wrote in a review column for *The Listener* that he did not propose to discuss American rock in 1977 at length, on the grounds that 'as viewers of the ossifying *Whistle Test* will vouchsafe, it has become tedious beyond belief'.[30] *The Old Grey Whistle Test* was BBC2's staple alternative to *Top of the Pops*, and while it featured a certain amount of new wave music, it remained true to its policy of being based on albums and album tracks rather than singles, keen not to shift its musical policy too suddenly. John's musical menu could include anything from Status Quo and Van der Graaf Generator to The Jam, The Boomtown Rats, and Siouxsie and the Banshees. It was his wholehearted endorsement of the latter that helped them to sign with a major label, in this case Polydor, and then find instant success on the singles and album charts.

However, 1977 was not only the year of punk rock. John was at the Vortex, Wardour Street, Soho, on 16 August 1977, where The Adverts and The Outsiders were playing. During a record break, a voice announced over the PA that Elvis Presley was dead. To his horror and that of other luminaries present (such as Jonathan Ross and Danny Baker), the crowd cheered and began jumping up and down, chanting in celebration. Baker was so angry that he leapt on stage, grabbed a microphone, and harangued the crowd, only to be hit by a bottle and then pulled off stage by Jimmy Pursey of Sham 69, who had the decency—unlike most of the other punks there—to fear genuinely for his safety. As Baker recovered backstage, bleeding and shaking, he looked up to see John with tears streaming down his face. Once he could talk, he thanked Baker for 'getting up there' and they left the club, thoroughly chastened.[31]

Despite this, John continued to champion punk and reggae. That year, the 'Festive Fifty' turned into a 'Festive Sixty' of his own personal favourites. The Motors' 'Dancing The Night Away' headed a list that also included records from Sham 69, John Cooper Clarke, The Clash, the Sex Pistols, and the reggae of Althea and Donna, as well as representatives from established acts like David Bowie, Status Quo, Dave Edmunds, and Little Feat. In 1978—the year of the last Peel sessions from pre-punk acts like Roy Harper, Rab Noakes, and Racing Cars—he returned to form with a listeners' chart, placing 'Anarchy in the UK' at No. 1, with The Clash and Stiff Little Fingers hot on their heels, and 'Stairway to Heaven' hanging on in at No. 14.

Years later, some remembered his championship of punk rock (played largely by white boys) and accused him of only playing white music. They had not done their research, seemingly unaware of his passion for reggae and hip hop. John retorted that he listened to music with absolutely no interest in the artist's race, colour, preference to breakfast foods, height, or shoe size. 'The only footling prejudice' he permitted himself was that any musicians whom he suspected of supporting Everton or Arsenal had 'a bugger of a time getting their ponderous tripe on to the programme'.[32]

The year 1978 would go down in the Peel Annals as the year that produced his favourite single of all time. When he first heard The Undertones' 'Teenage Kicks' that summer, he was completely blown away by it; after broadcasting it for the first time, he unapologetically played it again straight afterwards. Years later, he mused that 'after a few days of listening to sizzling new releases and worrying that the music was merging into a characterless soup', he would put it on again to remind himself exactly how a great record should sound.[33] Initially a self-financed release on the independent Belfast label Good Vibrations, it was promptly picked up by Sire Records. When John heard his daytime Radio 1 colleague Peter Powell playing it as his Record of the Week, he was so thrilled that he burst into tears.[34] He financed a session for the group in Belfast for broadcast that autumn, and when they came to England in January 1979 to support The Rezillos on tour, they did a second session for the show. People sometimes asked John why exactly he did his programme. He replied that he was not doing it for the credibility, the cool, the major record labels, or the music industry; 'I do it for people like The Undertones.'[35]

At around the same time, John Peel and John Walters found another group who would become an important part of the former's life—The Fall. His rather odd friendship with singer Mark E. Smith blossomed into a regular exchange of letters, but personal meetings between the two rarely went beyond a mumbled greeting and a gentle punch on the shoulder. They recorded the first of seventeen Peel sessions in May 1978, and he owned more records by them than any other artist, all kept in a special VIP enclosure, separated from the rest of his vast collection.[36] Another group of whom John approved were Altered Images, who were so grateful that they invited him to join them on one of their albums, adding backing vocals to a version of Neil Diamond's 'Song Sung Blue' on their 1982 album *Pinky Blue*.

By now, Chinnery and others had long since given up on trying to tame their station's most wayward presenter. In an interview published in October 1979, a few weeks after his fortieth birthday, Chinnery said the Corporation had left Peel 'to get on with it.' He was paid not to go off and work for a commercial radio station. 'I wouldn't want to go to one anyway,' John said, 'because they wouldn't let me do what the BBC let me do.'[37] Still, he never felt totally secure in his job. Gratifying as it was to keep winning polls as the best DJ in *New Musical Express* and *Melody Maker* year after year, if ever he failed to end up on top, his instant reaction was 'this is the end', anticipating that he would be supplanted by some eager rival from the younger generation. Nevertheless, as his wife recognised, if he had ever considered himself indispensable, his show might have gone downhill. He was so relieved to survive year after year that he would accept without demur the latest encroachment on his running time, much as his family were furious at the show forever being surreptitiously nipped and tucked.[38]

However, the fun of discovering all this new music came at a price. Aware of his importance as a DJ in breaking unsigned acts, eager young hopefuls sent him their demos on vinyl and tapes (and later CDs). Whenever he returned home from holiday, there would be another huge delivery to plough through.

John had a rather equivocal relationship with some of his fellow DJs on Radio 1. Apart from Jimmy Saville and Alan Freeman, most were several years younger than him. He got on very well with some, especially David Jensen, whom he called his 'Rhythm Pal' (or occasionally 'Kid Jerkin') and Janice Long, both of whom shared his musical tastes. Many of the others looked up to him in a manner perhaps best compared to that of cheery kids in the fifth form, somewhat in awe of the lofty, sharp-tongued upper-sixth former whose approval was not earned lightly, and who bestowed less-than-flattering nicknames on some of them. Dave Lee Travis was sometimes called 'Dickie Lee Torpid' on air, while Tony Blackburn was 'Timmy Bannockburn'. The former, Peel opined, was 'an otherwise likeable man' capable of reducing him to fury by perpetually referring to the BBC World Service as 'the BBC Wild Service'.[39] Tony Blackburn, who had opened Radio 1 with the first breakfast show in September 1967 and was initially renowned for his corny jokes, might not have always been the most publicly tolerant of individuals when it came to musical tastes. A few years later, he told a regional newspaper that he thought *Top Gear* should be axed because the bands Peel featured were 'hairy, scruffy individuals, unsociable towards everyone'.[40] Perhaps one should make allowances for the possibility that the journalist to whom he spoke had had a vested interest in twisting his words before filing his copy. Harsh—if exaggerated—words about colleagues on such a public medium as national pop radio undoubtedly helped to sell papers.

The men's animosity towards each other mellowed in later years, but their earlier relationship was often uneasy. Tony was annoyed when John, whom he thought looked upon him as the devil incarnate, took him to task in the press from time to time for no apparent reason. Yet whenever they met in private, Peel remarked graciously to him, 'People don't realise how much you've done for soul music.'

A flattered Blackburn could not resist replying, 'I bet you'd never say that publicly.' He felt John was a little jealous that Tony was built up as the face of Radio 1 in the early days, and that John's evening slot meant he was not part of the mainstream. 'He realised he wasn't as good as the rest of them on Top 40 radio,' Tony said. 'He was slow, his voice wasn't right for it.' John, he opined, 'was a clever man who captured a niche market', making a name for himself firstly on *The Perfumed Garden*, then with the BBC on *Top Gear* and his subsequent shows, even if his heart had not initially been in the less mainstream music. Tony later said, 'One day, [John] was sitting in the studio listening to this very odd music, and he said to me, "This is a load of shit, but I could make something out of it."' Tony contended that once John began working for the Corporation, 'he realised he could make a name for himself as an alternative DJ. He wasn't stupid, he knew what he was doing'.[41]

Among the daytime presenters, the one whom John respected most as a kindred spirit was Johnnie Walker, who, alongside Terry Wogan and Alan Freeman, was one of the few other Radio 1 presenters invited to John and Sheila's wedding in 1974. Johnnie later said that John never saw him as a grinning, 'Isn't this all fun?', 'shop-opening' DJ, and that they would exchange knowing and sympathetic glances at the truly embarrassing functions they were both obliged to attend over the years.[42]

When Bob Harris began working at Radio 1 in 1970, he and John initially got on well, but the relationship soured before long. John was also a friend of Sue, Bob's wife at the time, and when he felt Bob was proving a poor husband, John took to ignoring him. On one occasion, John walked past Bob in a corridor without speaking to him. Bob caught up with him and pulled him into an empty office, but John just stared impassively at the floor, refusing to tell Bob what the problem was. After that, neither man spoke to the other for almost twenty years, although they later made up.[43]

Peel found a good friend with the arrival at Radio 1 of Andy Kershaw, who would establish a name for himself as Radio 1's main world music presenter. Though twenty years younger, he established an instant rapport with the two Johns, Peel and Walters, and was thrilled to be falling into the same job and the same office as the man who had been his inspiration for so long. Even so, he and John later had their differences. Andy would be reluctant to polish John's halo, commenting that he featured a lot of rubbish in his shows that was 'played for being new *per se* rather than because it was any good', while also describing him as grumpy, disloyal, and almost insufferably paranoid.[44]

By this time, John was happy to combine his job with the role of a husband and father to his growing family. Home was now Peel Acres, a thatched cottage near Stowmarket, Suffolk, which housed his ever-growing record collection and a home studio from which he could broadcast many of his shows. In addition to pre-recorded sessions, he sometimes featured live performances—usually from the BBC Maida Vale Studios, but also on occasion from the living room at Peel Acres. This was meat and drink to the BBC, being less expensive to broadcast from Suffolk than Maida Vale. Acts such as Blur, PJ Harvey, and Cinerama were thrilled to arrive at the house in the afternoon and do a sound check before the evening show in these hallowed surroundings. Possibly no act was more appreciative than Belle and Sebastian. When they came to play, they presented Sheila with flowers and food, as well as toys for the dogs. For one session, they arrived with their own ingredients to make White Russians for everyone. Sheila was startled when they asked if they could use the fridge; her immediate reaction was, 'Why have they brought their own milk?' Once the vodka and Kahlua were produced, she realised what was in store. By the end of the evening, nobody was capable of speech or properly coordinated movement.[45]

During the shows broadcast from his house, John often affectionately mentioned Sheila and the children. All four—William Robert Anfield, Alexandra Mary Anfield, Thomas James Dalglish, and Florence Victoria Shankly—bore names reflecting his passion for Liverpool Football Club. Towards the end, Sheila also had her chance to become part of the show, presenting 'Pig's Big 78', a vintage record from any time during the first fifty years or so of the previous century. A selection of these appeared on a compilation CD, *The Pig's Big 78s—A Beginner's Guide*, in 2006.

Sometimes he would share his excitement and sorrow with listeners on the fluctuating fortunes of his favourite football team. On one occasion, Liverpool lost a particularly important game to Brighton & Hove Albion, also known as 'The Seagulls'. When John's technical operator arrived at Broadcasting House that evening to prepare for the show, John asked if he could produce some sound effects of seagulls and machine guns. The operator duly obliged, and at the top of the show, listeners were greeted not with a cheery 'Good evening and welcome', but the sound of screaming seagulls being apparently gunned down by unrelenting fire.

By 1980, the records John played gave the impression that he cared little for most chart music, but to every rule there was an exception. That summer he was particularly taken with Sheena Easton's '9 to 5', which he called 'a perfect pop record'. He sometimes played it on his roadshow during the next few years, provoking widely differing reactions. On one of his evening shows, he referred to fans of the song as the 'Sheena Barmy Army' and said that he earnestly hoped that when the John Peel Roadshow went out to do one of its 'awful' gigs and he played her record, everyone would chant 'SHEENA SHEENA' as they had done the last time, in Nottingham. At a roadshow in Southampton, however, the crowd let him down, just standing and staring at him as if to say, 'This man is a loony'. When he appeared on the 1982 Christmas Day special of *Top of the Pops*, he sported a Sheena Barmy Army sweatshirt.

John also admitted to liking Madonna records, and he and Sheila held a Madonna party for their daughter Alexandra's birthday one year, but he did not play them on his show 'as everybody else [did]'. In 1986, he attended a press conference for her film *Shanghai Surprise*, hosted by the ex-Beatle-turned-movie-producer George Harrison. It was a source of eternal regret for John that his nerves failed him when it came to asking for Madonna's autograph for his children; he was afraid people would think he was showing off.[46] Still, his admiration for her knew its bounds. After seeing her on stage at Wembley in August 1987, he concluded that she and her handlers had 'worked to make much of a modest talent', and suspected he 'was not alone in being disappointed by her performance'.[47]

John generally preferred to feature unsigned bands or those on independent labels, leaving them to the daytime shows once they became successful. Some of them might complain that he had left them behind, but he could argue that it was, in fact, the other way around. There was, he remarked, something in the process of becoming famous that removed from the music what he used to like: '... I don't know exactly what it is I like, but it's not there all of a sudden.'[48] The Sex Pistols' guitarist, Steve Jones, was angry when John called their later records 'substandard' and declined to play them on his show; John was unimpressed, not to say appalled, when the group reformed in 1996 for a few stadium dates.

Gradually, the mainstream pop world caught up with him—or perhaps it was the other way around. When he joined *Top of the Pops* as a regular presenter in February 1982, it was almost headline news. His straight-faced persona and dry wit made a stark contrast with the more effervescent approach of most of his colleagues. 'In case you're wondering who this funny old bloke is,' he explained almost apologetically to viewers who failed to recognise him at the start of the first show, 'I'm the one who comes on Radio 1 late at night and plays records made by sulky Belgian art students in basements dying of TB.' Sometimes he co-presented with David Jensen, whose Radio Luxembourg show, *Jensen's Dimensions*, he had keenly admired some ten years earlier. 'Welcome to another *TOTP*, we're the Burke and Hare of British Broadcasting,' was one of John's opening quips on behalf of them both. They had been friends ever since Jensen, formerly known as 'Kid' because of his youthful appearance, had joined Radio 1 in 1976. John was now genuinely pleased to be a part of a programme that he had once disdained, as he was not ashamed to admit. He was particularly flattered when one girl in the audience told him he was 'not a poser like all the others'. Jarvis Cocker of Pulp was one of many who admired his straight-faced demeanour in the middle of what was supposed to be a sometimes overdone party atmosphere.

Being John Peel, his on-screen patter often ruffled a few feathers. He might introduce a video of Queen with a reference to 'the Sun City boys', concerning their willingness to play in South Africa during the last days of apartheid. He might follow the chart-topping 'I Knew You Were Waiting For Me' by Aretha Franklin and George Michael with a comment that Aretha had such a fine voice that she could make any old rubbish sound good—'And I think she just has.' Once he followed a record with the words, 'And if that doesn't get to No. 1, I'm going to come and break wind in your kitchen,' reducing his co-presenter Janice Long to helpless laughter. Perhaps even funnier was the fact that somebody saw fit to inform the programme producer, Michael Hurll, who was in Australia at the time. He was awoken in the middle of the night, and, as Peel sardonically put it, 'alerted to this extraordinary danger to national security' engendered by his particular drollery. Yet he escaped censure for this and also for the moment when, alongside David Jensen on the eve of the June 1983 general election, he introduced 'Flashdance (What a Feeling)' by Irene Cara 'with a video made in a country which still had a steel industry'. It was the same incorrigible presenter who was known to sign off his show at the end of the night with a gruff, 'More of the same unpleasant and disorientating racket on tomorrow night's programme—until then, from me John Peel, goodnight and good riddance.'

While he loved discovering and playing music from new acts much of the time, there was still something of the endearing Luddite about him. 'I shall never come to terms with CDs,' he once said, bemoaning the new digital medium. 'There's something about records that's enormously satisfying.' When somebody tried to persuade him that CDs were far superior to vinyl as they did not have surface noise, he retorted, 'Listen, mate, "life" has surface noise.' On a visit to Dave Lee Travis's house, John went in pursuit of his record collection, but, to his astonishment, found no vinyl at all. When he asked why, the 'Hairy Cornflake' told him that he had copied everything he really liked onto tape so he could play it in the car. Such a confession was nothing short of sacrilege to a man whose home was a living shrine to thousands of albums and singles on vinyl—and many older discs on shellac as well. It must have seemed like the equivalent of a connoisseur of fine art or antique prints scanning his collection into a computer.

To the end, he was fascinated by records in their pure 7" format. He left an archive containing over 100,000 vinyl records and CDs, and a wooden box containing 143 singles and some doubles, representing a selection of personal favourites. Spanning an era from the early 1950s to the early 2000s, they excluded anything by The Fall—whose records were always kept in a separate collection—but comprised, jazz, blues, skiffle, rockabilly, soul, punk, gems issued on his Dandelion label, indie rock, reggae, and more. The Beatles were represented by a rare three-track maxi-single of songs from *Abbey Road*, released on the Melodiya label, while the rest of the list contained The Undertones, Status Quo, The Move, Sheena Easton, The Misunderstood, Don Covay, Elmore James, The White Stripes, John Walters' old outfit The Alan Price Set, Sam and Dave, and Nilsson, among others.

His adoration of good old-fashioned discs did not prevent the occasional hiccup on air. It was all too easy to play something at the wrong speed, and in an age when 7", 10", and 12" platters might be 33, 45, or even 78 rpm, any DJ would know mistakes were easily made. The sign that he had got it wrong again would be a *sotto voce*, 'Er… Talk among yourselves for a moment.' Alternatively, he would bluff his way out of it. A Siouxsie and the Banshees 45 inadvertently played once at 33 was 'a killer track either way'. There was a standing joke at Radio 1 that one day he would introduce a band on stage and put them on at the wrong speed.[49]

As his children would admit, 'he wasn't terrifically good with computers'. Like many of his generation, John could sometimes be confused by the relentless march of information technology. He was known to have deleted several thousand words of beautifully crafted prose at least once while coming to terms with his laptop. To the end of his days, he would type up session lists for the running orders on his programme on an old manual typewriter, having found a traditional stationers' shop in Thetford that still stocked ribbons, and fax it to his producer.[50] John's children would also gently complain about having a parent with such noisy tastes. On one occasion, he was playing music in his room when two of them came to him to ask if he could turn the music down as they could not hear the television. 'I'm supposed to say that to you,' was his reply.[51]

Dave Hill of *The Independent* once wrote:

[He was] the supreme national disc jockey, partly because of his immensely attractive radio persona—ironic, absurdist, self-deprecating—but also because of his partisanship and a singularity of taste which sometimes brims over into caprice.[52]

His readiness to play hardcore outfits like Napalm Death and the Electro Hippies, both of whom could boast at least one item in their catalogues lasting precisely one second, certainly demonstrated a singularity of taste. Yet while the vast majority of his show consisted of records from newer artists, there was still the occasional surprise in store. A devoted admirer of Roy Orbison, he approached the first Traveling Wilburys' album in 1988 with trepidation but soon found himself converted, especially by 'Not Alone Any More', a track written for Orbison that showcased his inimitable voice to perfection. When the singer died suddenly that December—ironically on the verge of a solo comeback—John said that he felt as if a window had been bricked up in his home, and he presented a moving, respectful tribute on Radio 1. Some eleven years later, he was on stage when Tony Bennett performed at the Glastonbury Festival. He and John Walters were so enraptured that they tried to book him for a session. Bennett was ready to oblige until he had to cry off with a bad throat. Commenting on the matter in a review, John referred to the band Nile, who specialised in death metal—'a form rarely essayed by Tony Bennett—although I'd like to hear him give it a go.'[53]

A more emotional side sometimes came through John's gruff, sometimes curmudgeonly exterior, and never more so than when tragedy struck at Hillsborough in April 1989. Ninety-six Liverpool fans were killed at an FA Cup semi-final through overcrowding on the terraces. Fellow Radio 1 DJ Nicky Campbell, whose evening show followed John's, called the first programme after the event a piece of broadcasting he would never forget. Unusually, he said nothing at the start of the show, instead playing Aretha Franklin's version of 'You'll Never Walk Alone'. Campbell looked through the glass from his adjacent studio and Peel was silently weeping, as were, he was sure, all his listeners. 'Nothing more needed to be said,' remarked Campbell.[54] John had been invited to the match, but he had not attended one since the Heysel disaster four years earlier, when he and his wife had been in the stadium as thirty-nine fans were crushed to death and over 600 injured while trying to leave. Since then, he admitted to finding 'crowds of any sort really scary'.

According to Sheila, John remained very shy throughout his life. Whenever they were invited to parties together, he would look for some little job to excuse him from the business of having to socialise with others. Having found something to do and occupy his attention, he would take as long as he could over it, even spending up to three hours doing the washing up or making cups of coffee while the party was going on in the next room. Sometimes people came over to him for a few words and then drifted away again, and on other occasions he would go unnoticed for the whole evening.[55]

In August 1989, his fiftieth birthday was marked by a revealing feature in *The Independent*. It announced that his show's audience figures had risen sharply since Radio 1 had begun broadcasting in stereo and he had been rescheduled from 10.00 p.m. to 12.00 midnight to mid-evening. He also remarked, with amusement, that his bosses had told him he would need to soften his approach a little, so he nodded and went on playing exactly what he had always done on the programme. They paid him another visit a month later and said, 'Well done—you've got it exactly right'. This, he felt, told him much about the way some people listened (or did not listen) to things. His enthusiasm remained undimmed:

> I think, all the time, that I'm enjoying music more than I ever have before. I sometimes feel guilty that it doesn't diminish. Most of my contemporaries gave up listening to anything new a long time ago. I can't understand why other people don't feel the way I do. It's like the old joke about everybody being out of step except our dad. I feel that's true. It's the others who are wrong, not me.[56]

While he always saw himself as a radio presenter and was uncomfortable with the medium of TV, he would still appear on the latter from time to time. As well as *Top of the Pops*, in the 1980s he was an occasional team member on *Pop Quiz*, presented by Mike Read, and presented BBC coverage of the Glastonbury Festival and other music events. One of his ultimate accolades came in December 1995, after he had finished presenting what would be his last-ever *Top of the Pops*. He thought his hosting duties on the show had come to an end in 1987, and he was pleased (if puzzled) to be invited back to reprise his old role for one evening eight years later. The reason became clear when he was ambushed at the end of the show by Michael Aspel and the big red book for *This is Your Life*. Shown on TV the following month, the programme also featured walk-on appearances from family, friends, and Radio 1 colleagues from over the years, and a filmed message from Richard Branson.

John could also be seen and heard on BBC2's humorous look at the irritations of modern life, *Grumpy Old Men*, as a presenter of the Channel 4 series *Classic Trains*, and providing a voice-over for documentaries such as BBC1's *Life of Grime*. However, TV could be an irritant to a man whose first love was and always would be radio. It irked him when the breakfast

DJs used to tell listeners what they could watch in the evening, when, as loyal Radio 1 jocks, they should really have advised their audiences to forget the television and listen to John Peel instead. Mentioning it to his colleagues only made them resentful.[57]

The mid-1990s saw John become a regular fixture on Radio 4. In January 1990 he was Sue Lawley's guest on *Desert Island Discs*, with a choice of records from The Undertones, The Fall, Misty in Roots, The Four Brothers, Jimmy Reed, Roy Orbison, Rachmaninov, and Handel. His last record was 'Zadok the Priest', as played at the coronation of King George VI in 1937. For all his iconoclasm, Peel had always greatly admired the King, mainly because of the way he overcame his stammer and shyness. He had been delighted at school to find a friend who owned a complete recording of the coronation ceremony, and he sometimes referred to his sense of sadness when, as a boy of twelve, he heard that the King had passed away.

His feelings towards the monarch's descendants were perhaps more equivocal. Coming face-to-face with Princess Margaret at a *Desert Island Discs*-related function, they both discussed briefly the occasions on which they had appeared as themselves in the long-running radio soap opera *The Archers*. Later, he noted dryly in an article for *The Guardian* that they were unlikely to meet again and talk of Ambridge, as he had 'initiated a low-key campaign to give the Stuarts another go at being the Royal Family, thereby allowing the present lot a century or two in the reserves to rediscover their form'.[58]

In 1995, he began to present a programme on Radio 4, *Offspring*, about children. Running for two years, it developed into a magazine-style documentary, *Home Truths*, focusing on everyday life in British families. He asked that it should be free from celebrities, as he found real-life stories from others more entertaining. Sometimes, in long breaks between recording links, he would curl up on the office floor, snoozing under the desk, or drop off in his chair. The first time the senior producer, Chris Berthoud, found him lying down in there, he was afraid there had been some ghastly accident. He later became used to showing people around the office, and pointing him out—'That person sleeping,' he would say, 'is John Peel.' John claimed that his ability to nod off anywhere at will had been acquired during his national service days, when he would have to sleep in the back of Army trucks.[59]

Two years earlier, in April 1993, John had become a Radio 1 daytime DJ again for a week, hosting the lunchtime show as a stand-in for Jakki Brambles. He followed the usual format of featuring records from the playlist, news, weather, and travel, but also had a say in the less mainstream choices of music he played the rest of the time. A few months later, when Matthew Bannister succeeded Johnny Beerling as Programme Controller of Radio 1, several of the well-established DJs left the station with varying degrees of assent, but John remained inviolate. There was speculation over the reasons for his longevity; some argued that it was because he came from what was known as a 'good family' and had received a public-school education, while others suggested it was due to his unpredictability and the fact that he deserved to be taken seriously. Whatever, the reason, it was clear that anybody who tried to dismiss him from Radio 1 would do so at their peril.

With typical self-deprecation, John considered himself to be a handy safety valve. Anybody who called in to complain about the safe and predictable nature of the station's playlist, he opined, could be reminded that they could always listen to Peel, as 'he [played] strange discs'. Moreover, he was working for Derek Chinnery, Programme Controller from 1978 to 1985, who disliked him but was persuaded to keep him on largely by John Walters. When the latter teamed up with Peel as his producer, it was the start of a harmonious working relationship and steady friendship that endured until Walters' retirement in 1991 and death ten years later. They often referred to themselves as being like a man and his dog, only each of them thought the other was the dog. Peel called him a brilliant debater, or rather arguer, who could always see through to the core of any argument, sink his teeth into it, and not let go. Controllers would 'get so fed up with arguing with Walters that they would just roll over'.[60] According to Mark Radcliffe, who was twenty years younger than both men but became a close friend from the younger generation of Radio 1 DJs, Walters saw his primary function as 'dealing with all the bullshit and politics so Peel could get on with the programmes uninterrupted'.[61]

A few months after Bannister's appointment, John Peel was ready to praise him for his strategy. The station had 'contrived to sound different without sounding as though it [was] being different for the sake of being different'; the listeners had respect (if not always affection) for the new names that had been brought in, and this engendered a new atmosphere that encouraged veterans such as Steve Wright and Nicky Campbell to reinvent themselves (although both soon left Radio 1). Within a couple of years, however, his airtime was being severely reduced due to the advent of new shows presented by others, and he felt he was being shunted around weekend schedules at family-unfriendly times, when his audience was least likely to listen. He saw that his enthusiasm had been misplaced, or at least premature, and 'he had been made weirdly complicit in his own downsizing', as he wrote to Bannister of his disappointment at losing yet more hours on air.[62] Nevertheless, no other radio station would have given him the *carte blanche* that the Beeb always handed him on the proverbial plate.

Having written sporadically for the BBC's weekly magazine *The Listener* from 1968 until its demise in 1991, and for *Radio Times* since the early 1970s, in 1993 he began a regular column for the latter that continued each week for the rest of his life. His wry observations of the world around him—not always connected with the music scene—always guaranteed a thoughtful read, and never more so than when he penned a heartfelt tribute to John Walters on Walters' death in 2001. Had he not become a disc jockey, he could have had a career in the world of journalism. One would have expected no less from a man who at school was noted for his 'long facetious essays' and achieved four passes in his General Certificate of Education at Ordinary level, including Divinity. He failed that subject by a mile, but he was given marks for writing all his answers in what he considered to be the style of Damon Runyon.[63]

Occasionally, his dry sense of humour unintentionally landed him in trouble. In August 1997, he light-heartedly compared the divorced Prince and Princess of Wales, the former's then companion and later wife, Camilla Parker-Bowles, and the latter's friend Dodi Fayed to the four characters in the children's TV series *The Teletubbies*. Ironically, the week that column appeared coincided with the death of the Princess and Fayed in a car crash in Paris, and he duly added an apology in the next issue of the magazine.[64]

Yet this episode and his apparent sympathy for the dispossessed Stuart line proved no impediment to being granted one of the ultimate accolades. Unlike some contemporaries in the music world who declared they would never accept a 'gong', in November 1998 Peel donned his suit and went to Buckingham Palace to receive the Order of the British Empire. To him, it was like going to a service in a church to which one did not belong. He was more forthright a year later, when a BBC national poll to name the 100 greatest Britons of all time placed him at No. 43. 'It's quite clearly bollocks,' he remarked, 'but in a way quite gratifying bollocks.'[65] He hated being called 'a national treasure', thinking that it made him 'sound like a ruined building covered in ivy'.[66]

His political allegiances never altered with time. Defying the general principle that people veered more to the right with age, he owned up to becoming politically angrier over the years, declaring that he would sooner cut his hands off than vote Conservative. Though he welcomed a change of government and the premiership of Tony Blair in May 1997, he rapidly became disillusioned with New Labour, especially with what he called its kowtowing to the regime of President Bush during the Iraq War, claiming he could not in all conscience vote for the party again.[67] When Blair visited Radio 1, he asked to meet John Peel and his colleagues, Mark Radcliffe and Marc Riley, who were sometimes known as 'Mark and Lard'. The latter were happy to oblige, but the moment Blair appeared, Peel vanished.

Later, he said that as a Labour supporter, he felt it would have been hypocritical of him to shake the hand of the man who had betrayed so many socialist principles.[68]

John had performed gigs on the university circuit with the John Peel Roadshow for some decades, but he eventually called a halt to the practice for a while. From the late 1990s onwards, he resumed occasional appearances at prestigious events like the Tribal Gathering dance festival and Big Chill extravaganza, and at the Sónar festival in Barcelona. At the first Tribal Gathering, Sheila noted that as he launched into his set at the turntables, he 'succeeded manfully in his ambition not to play the first record at the wrong speed', but the second was another matter. He had resolved to play not just run-of-the-mill dance music, but sounds people could dance to. His choice included The Fall (inevitably), African guitar-driven soukous, reggae, a bit of mixing featuring the BBC commentary for Kenny Dalglish's performance at the European Cup, and Status Quo; in his words, he wanted to go 'down, down, deeper 'n' down' in history as the man who played Quo at Tribal.[69]

Over the next few years, John would include vintage classics at his gigs, with 'In The Midnight Hour' and 'You'll Never Walk Alone' often taking pride of place. Like all the best DJs, he simply put on whatever he thought would get people out on the floor. Sheila dreaded him scuppering the crowd's goodwill at any moment by playing some happy hardcore and then killing it with a jig straight afterwards. Nevertheless, people danced all the same to what on paper looked like a wilful clash of musical genres. An eclectic selection of Peel favourites was immortalised on a compilation CD; in his words, the record was not supposed to be mood-enhancing—'if anything, it's mood-demolishing'.

With his constant ability to reinvent himself, John sometimes seemed ageless, but at the age of sixty-two after complaining of persistent tiredness, he was diagnosed with diabetes. The family had already had a near-brush with mortality when Sheila was hospitalised with a life-threatening brain haemorrhage in 1996. Now it was time to reflect on the past. People had been pressing him to write his autobiography for about thirty years, and the family had a room built at Peel Acres for that purpose. John promptly filled the room with records instead. Yet the idea of writing memoirs had already crossed his mind; some ten years or so beforehand, he had written to his literary agent, Cat Ledger, with a synopsis of the book he had in mind. He later seemed less convinced, admitting that every now and then he had an expensive lunch with an agent, but they thought him 'too lazy and there [were] too many records to play'.[70] In April 2003, he signed a contract for his book, *Margrave of the Marshes*, which he began shortly afterwards. It was completed by Sheila, who was assisted by Ryan

Gilbey. The portion that John wrote himself ended with a brief paragraph about his years in America during the mid-1960s, crossing the border into Mexico with a male friend in search of the latter's favourite brothel. In an introduction to the finished work, his children wrote that they felt it important his story should be finished, if only to make clear that he did not meet his wife, their mother, in such an establishment.[71]

Sadly, he did not live long enough to complete the book himself. During the late 1990s, John had said that he had considered the possibility of retiring as a DJ at the age of sixty-five—but only briefly. 'There may come a time when I can't find any new records that I like,' he said, 'and I certainly couldn't fake it—but at the moment I relish people putting their heads round the door and saying "You call that music?"'[72] He never mastered the art—or perhaps the curse—of growing old gracefully. He was asked if his tastes would change with age. 'I like to think that I'll be doing radio programmes in ten years' time and thinking a lot of the stuff I'm playing now is crap,' he replied.[73] As John Walters opined, 'The day Peel reaches puberty, we're all in trouble.'[74]

John was still presenting his show at the age of sixty-five, but possibly with mixed feelings. Andy Kershaw claimed that towards the end, John's relationship with the BBC bosses was increasingly fraught. There was no question of terminating his employment, but Andy thought he looked 'terrible'. He was angry at his programme being put back further into the night, from 11.00 p.m. to 1.00 a.m., and he felt marginalised, saying, 'It's killing me.'[75] Still, it was business as usual as he broadcast from his studio at Peel Acres at 11.00 p.m. on 14 October 2004, telling listeners that it was a full house, with everyone else watching television while he did his usual job at the end of the hall. The two-hour show included records by the Detroit Cobras, Frank Stokes, Dollhouse, and a session from Trencher; John signed off with an assurance that he would return, refreshed, at the beginning of November.

A few days later, he and Sheila left for a two-week working holiday in Peru. It was their chance to visit a country they had always wanted to see, and he would collect material for a travel feature for *The Daily Telegraph*—ironic, perhaps, considering his politics. A week after their arrival, on 25 October, they were having a drink at their hotel. Suddenly, John started talking with sadness about John Walters, who had died three years earlier. 'I miss him, you know,' he said. 'I miss ringing him up when there's something on telly. I haven't got another friend who does things like that. I wish I'd spent more time with him before he died.' Mark Radcliffe had noted that Peel and Walters seemed perfect together, and he believed that after the latter's death, John's life was never quite the same again.[76] With hindsight, Sheila found her husband's words 'almost unbearably ironic'.[77] About half an hour later, he collapsed due to a massive heart attack. He was taken to a local hospital, but the doctors there could not save his life.

Many were stunned at his sudden passing. Tributes came from performers and colleagues alike. Feargal Sharkey of The Undertones called him the 'single most important broadcaster we have ever known', while for Jarvis Cocker, in a world that was becoming ever more homogenised and pre-programmed, Peel championed the 'sore thumbs' of the music scene. He remarked, '… I really can't think of anyone who could have done it better or who's going to do it now he's gone.'[78]

John's took place at Bury St Edmunds on 12 November, attended by over 1,000 people. Eulogies were given by his brother, Alan, and fellow DJ Paul Gambaccini. The coffin was carried out of the church to the sound of 'Teenage Kicks'. A few years earlier, he had expressed a wish to be buried—though not at that stage—so his children could stand solemnly by his grave, thinking 'Get out of that one, you swine,'—which would be impossible if he had been cremated. He said that every night, at dusk, the trumpeters of the 5th Battalion King's Shropshire Light Infantry would play Misty In Roots' 'Mankind' over the grave, and that the words 'Teenage dreams, so hard to beat' would be inscribed on his gravestone.

Over the years, lasting tributes came at regular intervals. The new bands' stage at the Glastonbury Festival, formerly 'the new bands' tent', was renamed the John Peel Stage in 2005. The first John Peel Day was held on 13 October 2005, the anniversary of his last show. The BBC encouraged as many bands as possible to stage gigs to commemorate the date; over 500 were staged in Britain and overseas, including performances from big-name acts such as New Order and The Fall, as well as new and unsigned outfits. Some years later, blue plaques bearing John's name were unveiled at two former recording studios in Rochdale to mark his contribution to the local music industry. BBC Radio 6 Music also inaugurated the annual John Peel Lecture, and the Corporation announced that part of Broadcasting House, the Egton Wing (named after Radio 1's old home, Egton House), would be renamed the Peel Wing. At Heswall, his birthplace, the Ravenscroft Public House opened its doors, while the John Peel Centre for Creative Arts was launched in Stowmarket as a live venue for music and performance, and as a community meeting point.

Most notably, there were several compilation albums that bore his name. *John Peel: A Tribute* (2004) was one of the most eclectic, with music from the mid-1950s to the new millennium, from Elmore James and Lonnie Donegan through to Fairport Convention, The Bonzo Dog Doo Dah Band, New Order, and Orbital. Donations from sales went to John's favourite charities—The Salvation Army, the Kariandusi School Trust, and East Anglia Children's Hospices.

John Peel had spent a remarkable—if unsteady—life with the BBC. He was often regarded with suspicion by the management, venting his irritation at being shunted around between one time slot and another. However, unlike Johnnie Walker and Kenny Everett, he could seemingly get away with anything (within reason). His status was unique in that nobody ever sought to interfere with the contents of his programme, much as the top brass (and some of his audience) might deride some of his records as verging on the wilfully unlistenable. He was challenging, but rarely challenged enough to be threatened. There never was another broadcaster quite like him, and there is unlikely to be another in the future. Perhaps the last word on John should go to a sound engineer who regularly worked for him at the BBC. She commented that there was something about him that brought out more affection—not only from the public, but also from the people he worked with—than she had seen with any other DJ or presenter before or since.

4
Tommy Vance

Hard rock and heavy metal are genres that have never really been cool or fashionable (except briefly during the early 1970s), and as such they have often had a bad press. Nevertheless, they also had their supporters over the years, and none more so than the man who flew the flag for the genre on BBC Radio for fifteen years, Tommy Vance. His passion for the music often masked the eclecticism of a very versatile and well-informed presenter, the possessor of one of the outstanding voices in broadcasting history.

Richard Anthony Crispian Francis Prew Hope-Weston was born on 11 July 1940 in Eynsham, Oxfordshire. His father was an electronics engineer, his mother a professional singer and dancer, and one of his grandmothers owned a travelling repertory company. After Richard was expelled from school for persistent non-attendance, he was employed briefly as a trainee manager at the Hyde Park Hotel. This was evidently no more to his taste than school, and at sixteen he ran away to join the Merchant Navy as a caterer—but he was soon discharged. He then enrolled as a student in Belfast, where he joined the Ulster Bridge Repertory Company, run by the actor James Ellis, and became a stage manager.

Like many of his generation in Britain, Richard had grown up with a love of pop and rock music, but he was less enamoured with the rather staid broadcasting style of the BBC Light Programme. Once he heard the pirates, and after he was introduced to the more brash sound of American commercial radio during his time as a cabin boy in the merchant navy, he knew that was what he wanted to do. From then on, his ambition was to become a DJ. He had once thought of being a musician, but lack of ability—or, rather, belief in his abilities—held him back. He was employed in radio, he later said, because he loved music, but knew he was no musician:

> I'm a failed drummer! I really wish I could play! But I can't, and I believe my voice is my instrument. I wouldn't get on stage or anything, though I was in pantomime when I was four ... I would just like to play every goddamn instrument there is![1]

For a time he worked as a mechanic for a jukebox company so he could hear music for nothing, despite the poor pay. Saving up his money, he bought a one-way ticket to Virginia; he crossed the Atlantic and took to the road in his ancient Chevy, travelling to Vancouver. One reason was so that he could be with his then-girlfriend, and the other was to explore any possible radio opportunities there. He auditioned unsuccessfully for several different stations while volunteering to help out in any way he could for the experience. At first, he was just a dogsbody at Radio CKUX for Jim Thom, who presented a show comprising comedy half-hours and request spots. Richard was responsible for fetching records from the library for Jim. When not helping out, he was allowed to practise in the empty studios, honing his craft; he watched the other jocks, learning from them, studying their delivery and making sure that absolutely every word he said between records counted. Soon he was given a show on the midnight to 6.00 a.m. shift.

At this time he called himself Rick West—coincidentally, also the showbusiness name of Tremeloes' guitarist Richard Westwood. Soon, however, the presenter would have a new identity. When Richard applied for a job at the KOL radio station in Seattle, he was informed that the young DJ who was originally going to take the job would be known as 'Tommy Vance'. The station had already recorded and aired an expensive set of jingles for him, some featuring The Johnny Mann Singers, but the DJ had failed to show up, so they asked Richard if he was prepared to take on the role under that name. When they showed him the contract and the rate of pay, Richard did not think twice. If they wanted to pay him that amount of money, he allegedly told the station staff, they could call him 'Judas Iscariot' for all he cared. Somewhere in the world, there is (or was) another man who would have been known as Tommy Vance.

While the former Hope-Weston was working at KOL, the first British DJ on the roster, he was offered the chance to move to Los Angeles and join a new station, KHJ. He tried to leave KOL at once, and when they would not release him, he sued them for breach of contract, contending that he was fraudulently induced to sign a contract, that the station was exploiting him, and that his chances of advancement had been destroyed. The court ruled that his contract was valid, and he was restrained from broadcasting for any other station other than KOL until it expired.

By October 1965 he was at last free to join KHJ, by then one of the most successful and influential Top 40 stations of the time. A claim that he knew The Beatles and had jammed with The Rolling Stones did his chances no harm at all, and he was put in charge of the 6.00 to 9.00 p.m. slot. He also dallied briefly with the idea of becoming a performer himself, taping a few songs at Goldstar Studios, Los Angeles, on a four-track recorder.

They were made with the same orchestra that used to play on most of Phil Spector's productions, featuring Glen Campbell on guitar. After being kept in the can for about a year, two of his singles were released on Columbia in September and November 1966. Songs written by Mick Jagger and Keith Richards, 'You Must Be The One' and 'Off The Hook', were the A-sides. Nine years later, a cover version of 'Silhouettes', a hit for The Rays and Herman's Hermits, appeared on Bell under the name of 'Shades'. The B-sides, Vance said, were 'recorded in five minutes in Bond Street'. In later years, he admitted to having made about eight singles altogether, maybe more, mostly under different names. When asked further about them, he seemed less than enthusiastic about providing more details.

As much as Tommy loved America, he decided to return home when he received his draft papers from the US Army and was asked whether he would like to go to Vietnam. The musician Ian Whitcomb lent him the fare and he flew to Seattle, crossing the border into Canada and then flying directly to London shortly before Christmas 1965. Getting off the plane with £47 in his pocket, he went straight to Radio Caroline's London office with a tape of his last Los Angeles programme. When a member of staff said they loved the tape and told him to come back after Christmas, he took a room in a Baker Street hotel. He returned to Radio Caroline when the office reopened, and a day later he was on his way to the ship in the North Sea. Going there from Los Angeles in five and a half days was the biggest culture shock of his life.[2]

Fortunately, the programme controller, Bill Hearne, was eager to employ a British DJ with American experience, and on 3 January 1966 Tommy presented his first show on Caroline South. The strapline was 'TV On The Radio', with Jack Constanzo's 'Naked City Theme' as his signature tune. While he relished the challenge of working somewhere new—and with the shadow of serving in Vietnam now removed—it meant a substantial drop in income, as he had been earning good money in America but now took home around £18.10s (£18.50) per week. He left Caroline and moved to Radio Luxembourg after about three months. His first marriage did not last, partly because his absences at sea had put too much of a strain on the relationship. When Ronan O'Rahilly of Radio Caroline invited him back to the ship *Mi Amigo* in December 1966, he eagerly accepted the offer.

For Tommy, and for the rest of the team, working at sea was tremendous fun. His first impression when he joined was that he had come to a lunatic asylum, and his second was that everybody was incredibly friendly. He recalled that there was no backbiting, no bitching, no politics—and an endless supply of liquid refreshment. He recalled, 'The typical day revolved around your air shift, whatever time you had to be on the air [and] around how much Heineken you'd had the night before.'[3] Of course, there were minor technical problems. The boat rocked, literally, and sometimes they had to put a half-crown on the tone arm to ensure the stylus tracked the record properly.

A very private man, Tommy spoke very little about his personal life to anybody except his closest friends. After the end of his first marriage, he married Susan Hanson, one of the stars in *Crossroads*. Years later, he told journalist Mick Wall that they were 'the Posh and Becks' of the day', living the celebrity life, hanging out with Jimi Hendrix, and 'making the scene in London'. It ended when he 'came home one day and she'd taken all the furniture'.[4] Later she married Carl Wayne, former vocalist with The Move.

Early the following year, it was known that the Labour government intended to pass the Marine Offences Bill, making the offshore radio stations illegal. The pirates and their legal advisors tried to find loopholes that would permit them to continue broadcasting lawfully, but they failed. Tommy was led to believe that Philip Birch, who was in charge of Radio London, was planning to move his station's operations to France, and if so, Tommy wanted to be there.

In July 1967, Radio London programme director Alan Keen persuaded Tommy to come aboard the *Galaxy*. He was already a devoted listener to 'Big L', and in particular a fan of John Peel's *Perfumed Garden* since his days on board *Mi Amigo*. Technical considerations made it difficult for him to hear the show well; the pirate ships were so physically close to each other that the output on Radio London's powerful transmitter swamped the receiver on Caroline and distorted the sound badly.

Radio London was undergoing an acute staff shortage because so many DJs were leaving before the Marine Offences Bill came into effect in August. Tommy pinned his hopes on the management's plans for relocation to France or elsewhere in Europe—hopes not shared by most of the other presenters—and was persuaded to join the station. He was one of the last to do so. He presented his first show on 25 July, the day he arrived on board. He was also at the microphone for the final Fab 40 on 6 August and the breakfast show the following morning, leaving the ship a day after that. His voice was heard on the last day of broadcasting, 14 August, when a pre-recorded programme was broadcast between 1.30 and 2.00 p.m. At the end of the show, Tommy and his co-host, Lee Peters, said a personal farewell to their audience.

The DJs who had not shared their management's optimism about continuing to broadcast from Europe were proved correct. Big L never found a base on the continent and chose to remain within the law by closing down on time. As he listened onshore to the final broadcast, Tommy felt dejected:

> It was very sad because it was a part of your life. I was perpetually confused by the evolution of the medium in this country because I'd

come from America, where radio was commonplace. It always struck me as terribly strange that if America had this proliferation of radio, why couldn't the UK have it?[5]

Like so many of his offshore colleagues, Tommy landed on his feet at Broadcasting House, and he was part of the original Radio 1 line-up when it opened on 30 September 1967. After the pirates, the BBC could hardly have been more different; Tommy found it 'had a certain discipline that you had to adhere to and a system that you had to grasp, which was no bad thing'.[6]

He could be heard for a few weeks as the co-presenter of the weekend afternoon show, *Top Gear,* with John Peel, until the latter was left as the sole host when the programme was shortened. Like other DJs, he also found a job (if only in the short term) as a television presenter. For a few weeks between May and July 1968, he compered *New Faces,* a fifteen-minute talent-spotting show from Granada TV, shown in the early Friday evening spot.

After that, he worked on occasional Radio 1 slots, including the new release showcase *What's New, Sounds of the Seventies* (a show launched in April 1970 and presented by several of the Radio 1 team in turn), and *Radio 1 Club* (a lunchtime show launched in October 1968 and replaced five years later by the *Radio 1 Roadshow*). He made a debut on BBC television ('TV' on the TV, in fact) as presenter of the first series of *Disco 2,* a late-night rock programme that ran for almost two years and was a forerunner of the more long-lived *The Old Grey Whistle Test*. The quality of that distinctive voice was beginning to be recognised, and he could be heard on Radio Caroline in commercials for Major Minor Records, a label set up by Phil Solomon, one of the station's directors. Tommy was soon in demand for television advertisements as well. He had a brief voice-only role as an announcer in one episode of the BBC situation comedy *Steptoe and Son* in 1972, and also worked as a continuity announcer for BBC2 television. It was said that he never became one of the front rank of presenters partly because of a lack of interest in celebrity status, and partly because he was not yet seen as being quite as musically-orientated as John Peel—and, as everyone recognised, there was only room for one John Peel. There was another place for him on the BBC World Service, on which he presented the weekly *Pop Club*.

Hankering after the challenge of something new, he joined Radio Monte Carlo International with two other DJs who had been on Radio 1 in its early days, Dave Cash and Kenny Everett. In 1973, all three joined the new London-based Capital Radio, the first legal commercial pop station to broadcast on mainland Britain. For a while, he co-hosted the three-hour morning show with Joan Shenton, a former interviewer, reporter, and presenter with BBC TV's *Nationwide* and then similar news programmes on Thames TV. Tommy and Joan were very different broadcasters; as he said, she was a former reporter and an intellectual, while he was the 'Hi, there, happy good morning' type. 'It was a strange marriage,' he recalled, 'but I vividly remember the honeymoon.' Later he played reggae and soul music on a weekend show.

The Vance voice was also employed in another, rather unusual format. Kenny Everett used to present a regular feature, *Moment of Terror*, on Capital. It consisted of a spoof horror story. One night, after both men had drunk a generous amount of wine, Kenny remembered he had to record a trailer for the show. Needing an appropriately horrific sound effect, Tommy obliged with a magnificent belch that they recorded through a Copicat—a machine that created repeating delay effects—with the tape loop set to slow. The result, enhanced by a large amount of echo and promptly dubbed 'the thing that ate Birmingham', reduced them to helpless laughter. Never one to waste a good idea, Kenny kept the sound and later used it again in his space serial *Captain Kremmen*. Tommy also had a more conventional role as 'DJ Ricky Storm' in Slade's feature movie *Flame* in 1975, in addition to a brief stint the following year on the Portsmouth station Radio Victory. He also became part of the British Forces Broadcasting Service team, presenting regular shows featuring interviews with guests and a mix of current pop. As it was his policy to record several shows one after the other, he found it useful to place a sign relating to the day of transmission on his desk while recording so that he could connect with the correct day of broadcast on the overseas stations.

In July 1977, Tommy recorded an interview with Johnny Rotten; the programme in which it aired would become his most famous with Capital. The Sex Pistols frontman and his group may have killed Bill Grundy's career stone dead, but when faced with a genuinely perceptive interviewer, Rotten proved a more articulate personality than the tabloids gave him credit for. Tommy gave him a chance to talk about his eclectic tastes and love of music. His mere presence on the show incurred the wrath of the Pistols' manager, Malcolm McLaren, who had never wanted him to do it in the first place. This was possibly because McLaren did not want his protégé to show himself up as a genuinely thoughtful individual, far removed from the spiky-haired, supposedly inarticulate public nuisance of popular legend. Accompanied by a selection of songs from David Bowie, Gary Glitter, Tim Buckley, Augustus Pablo, Captain Beefheart, and Peter Hammill, the interview was an unfailingly interesting and good-humoured exchange throughout. At one point, Rotten laughed as he admitted that he hated talking into a microphone. Tommy quipped consolingly, 'I sometimes get the same feeling, but it's the only way to do the radio business.' They found common ground in their love of reggae music, Tommy saying that in his case, it was mainly because for a long time he thought it was pretty much the only genre in which people were trying to do different things. When he said he had never seen anybody with a large pile of reggae records who was 'in, ostensibly, a white band', Rotten responded with a smile, 'Come round my place sometime!'[7] Few other DJs could have handled an interview as sensitively at such a time, or got the best out of the artist otherwise known as John Lydon. Tommy always remained proud of it, as one kindred enthusiast chatting to another:

> He [Rotten] took me for what I was, and I took him for what he was ... I think the music business, like anything else, even disc jockeys, needs a good kick up the arse every now and then. I like Rotten's ideals. I LOVE what he did to Bill Grundy, because Bill Grundy deserved that![8]

In view of a career-long history of regular switches from one station to another, it was perhaps not surprising that Tommy should eventually return to Radio 1; as a result, he once more became a regular on television.

The much-loved Saturday rock show hosted by Alan Freeman, Vance's long-time hero, came to an end in August 1978. Rock fans who found a vacuum in the schedules did not have to wait long for the mantle to be assumed by someone else. It was ironic that Fluff's slot had been axed allegedly because it was viewed as a minority taste, and yet the genre was granted what amounted to a replacement show only three months later. On 24 November 1978, Radio 1 welcomed the first of a fourteen-year run of what would become a broadcasting institution—*The Friday Rock Show*. With the aid of his researcher, Jon Kutner, Tommy spent a day each week choosing music for the two-hour show, which initially aired on Friday nights between 10.00 p.m. and midnight. Topped and tailed by the Dixie Dregs' instrumental 'Take it Off the Top', the programme was a selection of album tracks past and present—in Tommy's words, 'classic cuts'—plus studio sessions or live performances from contemporary groups and recordings from the BBC archives. In between was that endearingly familiar gravelly voice, 'The Music Vendor', proclaiming himself 'TV on the radio'. It was said that Tommy's vocal cords had acquired an extra timbre after years of cigar smoking. When he was advised by doctors to quit, he switched to Gitanes.

The show was not welcomed by John Peel, who took less than kindly to losing his Friday slot. In November 1978, Radio 1, which had been broadcasting on 247 metres medium wave, was moved to 275 and 285 metres. John Peel was to be moved to mid-evening, with David Jensen

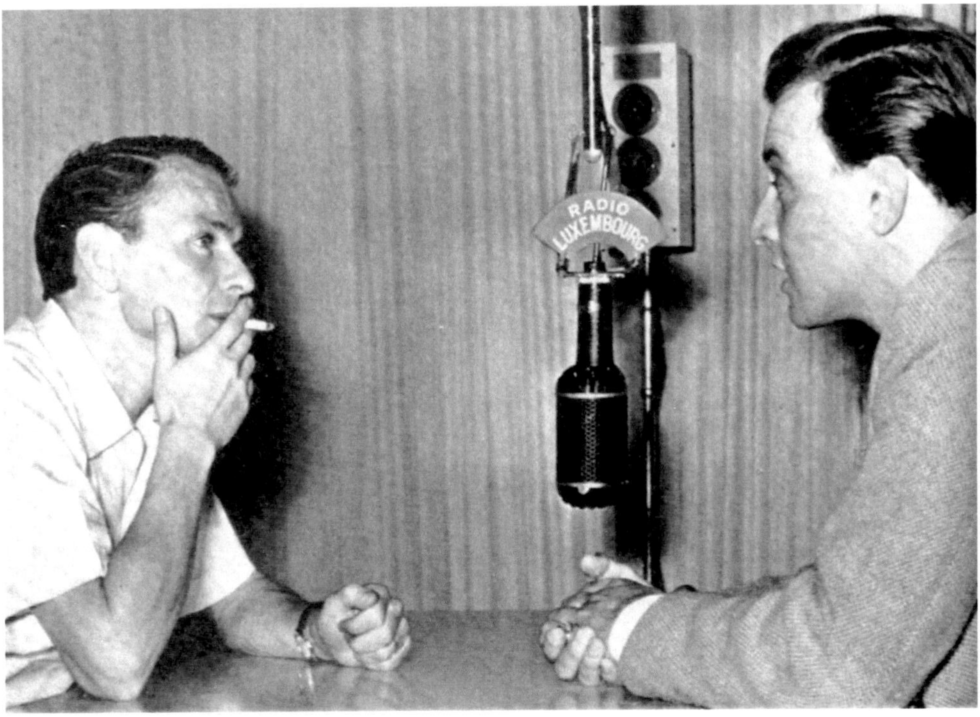

David Jacobs interviewing Frank Sinatra at Radio Luxembourg Studios, *c.* 1956.

Alan Freeman, Pete Murray, David Jacobs, and Jimmy Savile, the original *Top of the Pops* presenters, *c.* 1964. (*Trinity Mirror/Mirrorpix/Alamy Stock Photo*)

David Jacobs with The Beatles on the set of *Juke Box Jury*, December 1963. (*Trinity Mirror/Mirrorpix/Alamy Stock Photo*)

Below left: David Jacobs, *c.* 1990.

Below right: A frail David Jacobs outside the BBC studios in his last years as a presenter. (*Simon Matthews/Alamy Stock Photo*)

Alan Freeman with Dolores Gray and Barbara Windsor on the set of *Juke Box Jury*, April 1963.

'Madison Time', a single by Alan Freeman, released in November 1962.

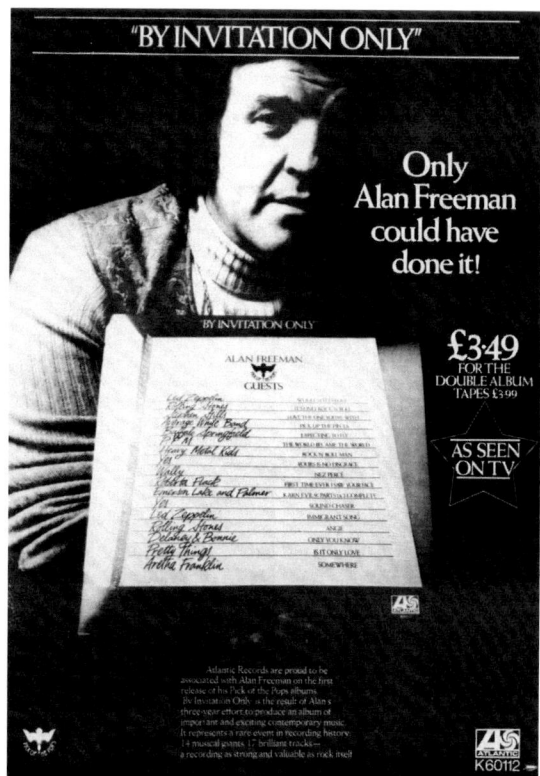

A press advertisement for Alan Freeman's compilation album *By Invitation Only* (1976).

The Radio 1 DJs celebrating the tenth anniversary of Radio 1, 1977. *From left to right*: Alan Freeman, Dave Lee Travis, Paul Gambaccini, Paul Burnett, David 'Kid' Jensen, and Tony Blackburn. (*Trinity Mirror/Mirrorpix/Alamy Stock Photo*)

Alan Freeman interviewed by *Nova Lepidoptera*, the Barclay James Harvest fanzine (1988). (*K. and M. Domone*)

Alan Freeman and Chris Tarrant with Status Quo, celebrating the group's twenty-fifth anniversary at Butlins Holiday Camp, Minehead, October 1990. (*Theodore Liasi/Alamy Stock Photo*)

Left: John Peel, 1968. (*Trinity Mirror/Mirrorpix/Alamy Stock Photo*)

Below: The Radio 1 DJs outside Broadcasting House shortly before the station's first anniversary, 1968. *Back row, left to right*: John Peel, David Symonds, Dave Cash, Stuart Henry, Johnny Moran, Alan Freeman. *Middle row, left to right*: Pete Myers, Mike Raven, Terry Wogan, Keith Skues, Kenny Everett (almost hidden), Ed Stewart. *Front, left to right*: Barry Aldiss, Chris Denning, Robin Scott (Station Controller), Tony Blackburn, Sam Costa (Radio 2 DJ).
(*Trinity Mirror/Mirrorpix/Alamy Stock Photo*)

Right: John and Sheila, the newly-married Mr and Mrs Ravenscroft, and Woggle, their bridesmaid, August 1974. (*Trinity Mirror/Mirrorpix/Alamy Stock Photo*)

Below: John Peel and Woggle, his Old English Sheepdog, 1972. (*Trinity Mirror/Mirrorpix/Alamy Stock Photo*)

Above left: Steve Lamacq and John Peel at the decks of Subcity Radio, Glasgow, March 1997.
(*Trinity Mirror/Mirrorpix/Alamy Stock Photo*)

Above right: John Peel backstage at Glastonbury Festival, 2004.
(*Edd Westmacott/Alamy Stock Photo*)

Radio Caroline DJs in the mess of *Mi Amigo c.* November 1966. *Left to right*: Tommy Vance, Steve Young, Mike Ahern, Robbie Dale, John Aston, Johnnie Walker.
(*Keith Humphries*)

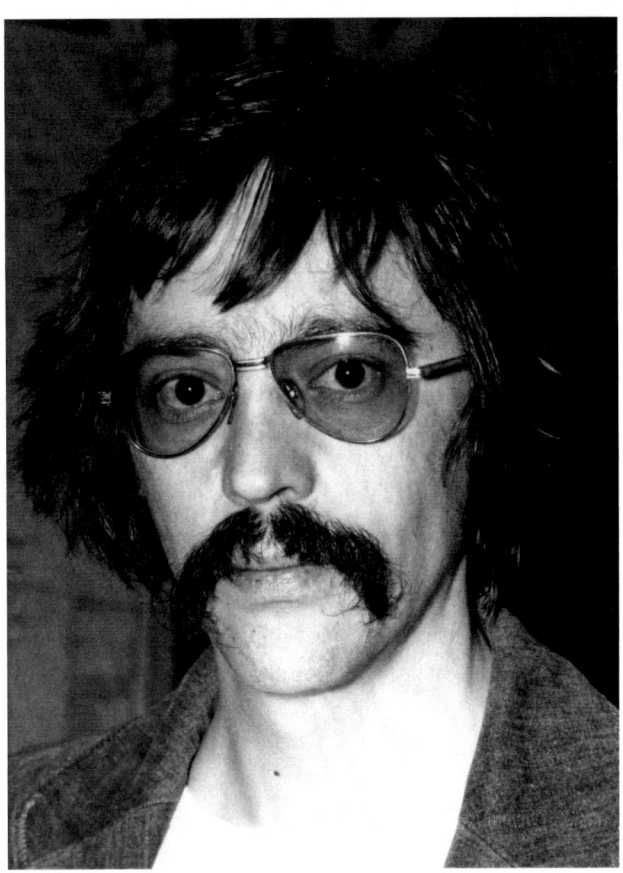

Tommy Vance, 1973.

Nicky Horne, Tommy Vance, Tony Myatt, and Roger Scott clowning around at Capital Radio, *c.* 1976.

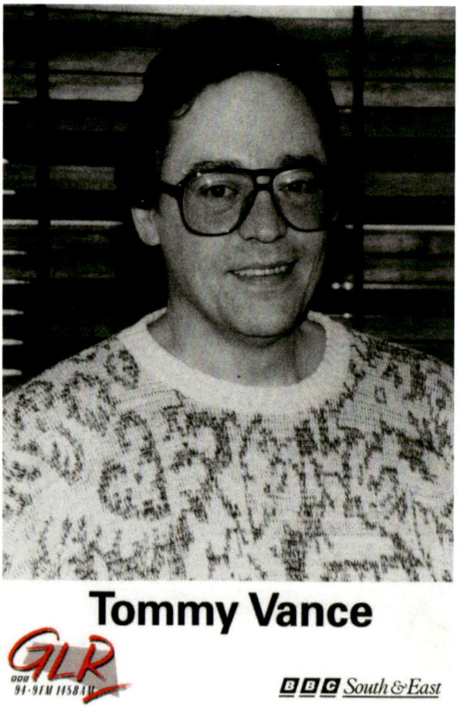

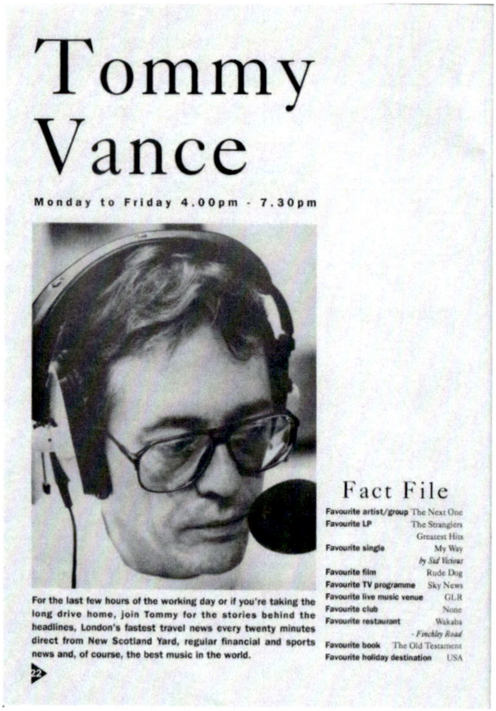

Tommy Vance

Monday to Friday 4.00pm - 7.30pm

For the last few hours of the working day or if you're taking the long drive home, join Tommy for the stories behind the headlines, London's fastest travel news every twenty minutes direct from New Scotland Yard, regular financial and sports news and, of course, the best music in the world.

22

Fact File

Favourite artist/group	The Next One
Favourite LP	The Stranglers Greatest Hits
Favourite single	My Way *by Sid Vicious*
Favourite film	Rude Dog
Favourite TV programme	Sky News
Favourite live music venue	GLR
Favourite club	None
Favourite restaurant	Wakaba *- Finchley Road*
Favourite book	The Old Testament
Favourite holiday destination	USA

Above left and right: Tommy Vance at Greater London Radio (GLR).

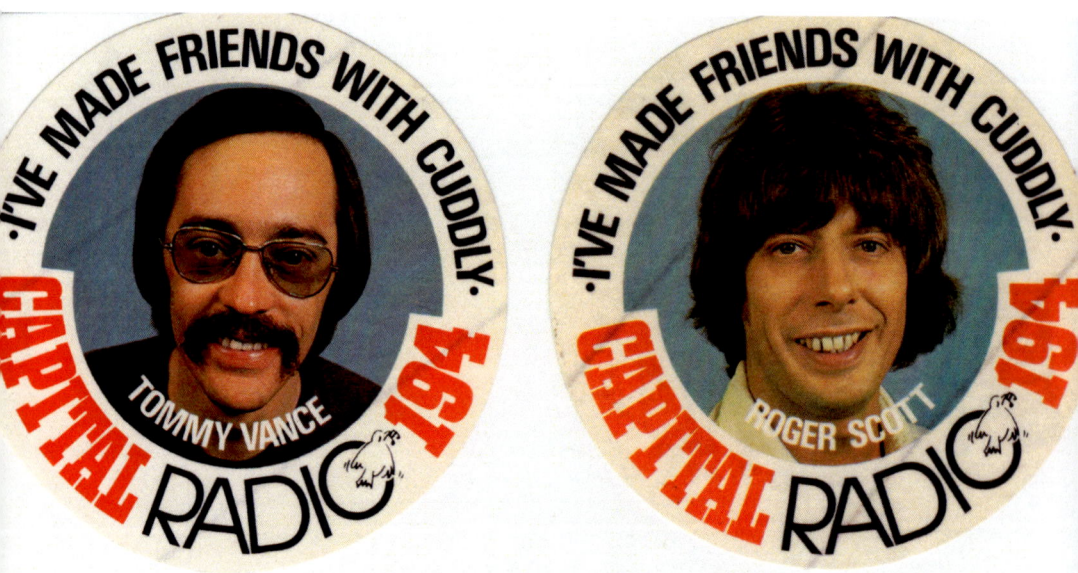

Capital Radio promotional stickers featuring Tommy Vance and Roger Scott.

Tommy Vance with Pat Sharp, Mike Read, 'Curlyman', and Nicky Horne at the launch of Cable TV, a short-lived music channel run out of Molinare, Soho, *c.* 1982.

Tommy Vance (in sunglasses) with Johnnie Walker, Rohan O'Rahilly of Radio Caroline, Dave Lee Travis (in back row), and others at the thirty-fifth-anniversary Offshore Reunion, Radio London, August 2002. (*Chris Payne*)

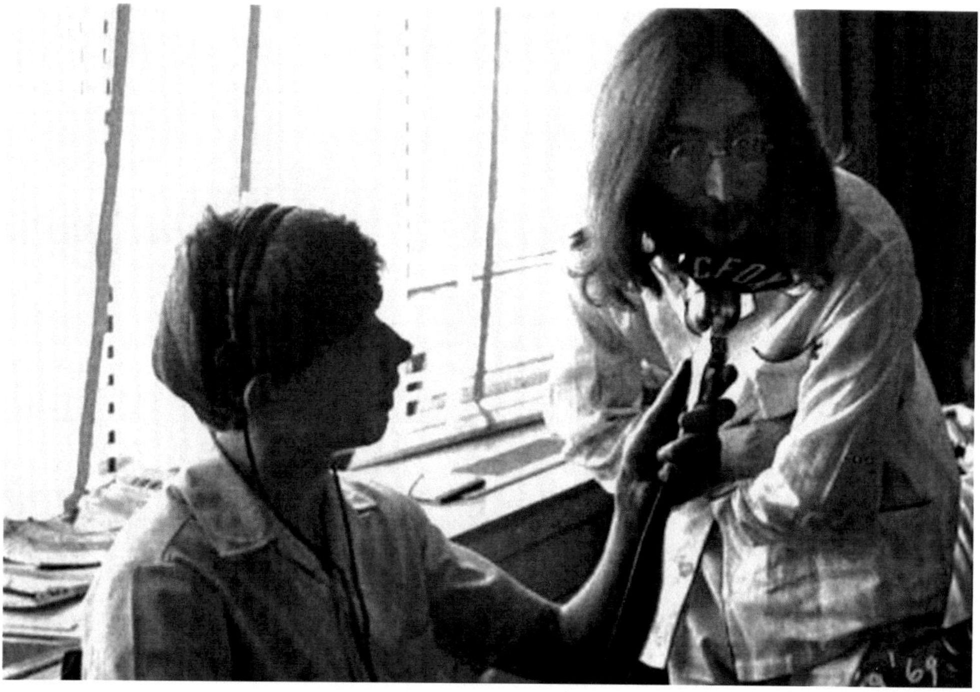

Above: Roger Scott interviewing John Lennon for CFOX Montreal at the time of the 'Bed-In For Peace', May 1969. (*Shown with the permission of Marc Denis, 1470 CFOX Montreal Radio Archive, marcdenis.com/cfox*).

Below: Roger Scott at the Global Village. (*Jamie Scott*)

Right and below: Roger Scott at Capital Radio. (*Jamie Scott*)

CFOX NOW 30

FRIDAY - JUNE 6th - 1969

5	1	LOVE THEME FROM ROMEO & JULIET	HENRY MANCINI	RCA VICTOR 0131
1	2	Love (Can Make You Happy)	Mercy	Columbia 2875
2	3	Bad Moon Rising	Creedence Clearwater Revival	Fantasy 622
3	4	Baby I Love You	Andy Kim	Steed 716
9	5	No No No No	Danish Lost and Found	Barry 3503
7	6	Grazin' In the Grass	Friends of Distinction	RCA Victor 0131
3	7	Oh Happy Day	Edwin Hawkins Singers	Pavillion 20001
4	8	Get Back/Don't Let Me Down	The Beatles	Apple 2490
20	9	Proud Mary	Solomon Burke	Bell 783
15	10	What is a Man	Four Tops	Motown 1147
6	11	Gitarzan	Ray Stevens	Monument 1131
14	12	Ram Jam	Byron Lee	Jad 1038
**	13	THE BALLAD OF JOHN AND YOKO	THE BEATLES	APPLE 2531
27	14	In the Ghetto	Elvis Presley	RCA Victor 9741
11	15	Marley Purt Drive	Jose Feliciano	RCA Victor 9739
13	16	Nothing But a Heartache	The Flirtations	Deram 85038
29	17	It's Never Too Late	Steppenwolf	Dunhill 4192
18	18	Hands of the Clock	Life	Polydor 540.009
19	19	When I Die	Motherlode	Revolver 002
26	20	Happy Heart	Andy Williams	Columbia 44818
21	21	I Threw it all Away	Bob Dylan	Columbia 44826
22	22	My Cherie Amour	Stevie Wonder	Tamla 54180
23	23	Where's the Playground Susie	Glen Campbell	Capitol 2492
28	24	Manhattan Spiritual	Sandy Nelson	Imperial 66375
25	25	The April Fools	Dionne Warwick	Scepter 12249
**	26	ISRAELITES	DESMOND DECKER & THE ACES	UNI 55129
30	27	Let Me	Paul Revere	Columbia 44854
**	28	MY PLEDGE OF LOVE	JOE JEFFREY GROUP	WAND 11200
**	29	GOOD MORNING STARSHINE	OLIVER	JUBILEE 5659
**	30	WHILE YOU'RE OUT LOOKING FOR SUGAR	THE HONEY CONE	HOT WAX 6901

CFOX - PICK ALBUM

THE AGE OF AQUARIUS — THE FIFTH DIMENSION — SOUL CITY SCS 92005

CHARLES P. | JOHN & YOKO | JOHN & YOKO | ROGER SCOTT

The CFOX Now 30 Chart, 6 June 1969, with John Lennon and Yoko Ono, and DJs Charles P. Rodney Chandler and Roger Scott. (*Shown with the permission of Marc Denis, 1470 CFOX Montreal Radio Archive, marcdenis.com/cfox*)

'Roger Scott: Music Power'; a Capital Radio promotional flyer.

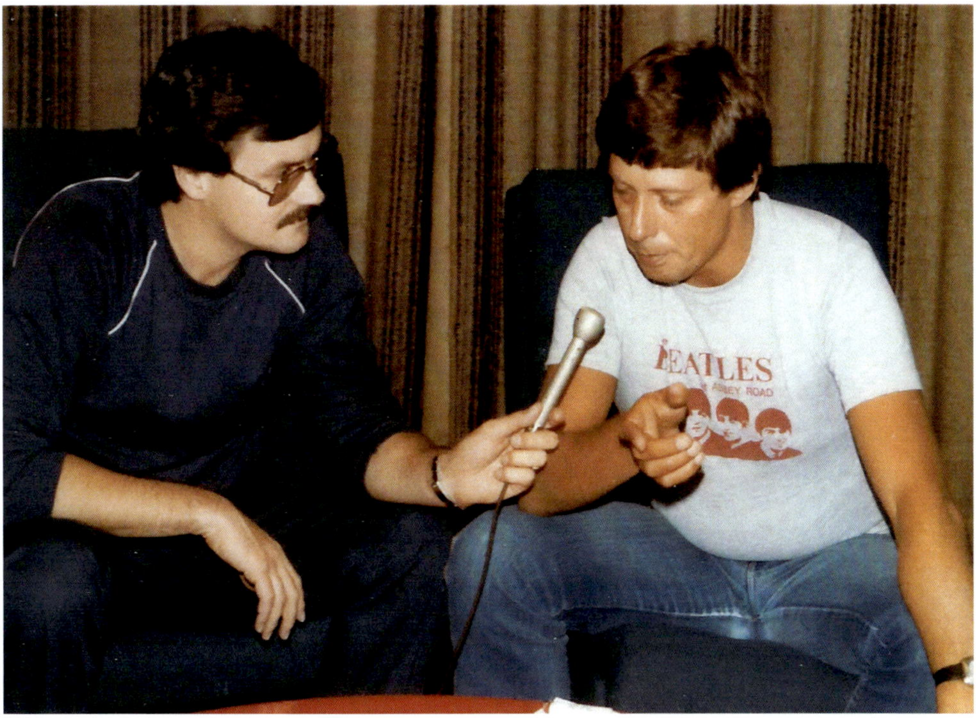

Marc Denis and Roger Scott at Capital Radio, September 1983. (*Shown with the permission of Marc Denis, 1470 CFOX Montreal Radio Archive, marcdenis.com/cfox*)

Roger Scott and Lesley-Ann Jones, Florida, August 1989. (*Lesley-Ann Jones*)

Friends and guests at a celebration of the life of Roger Scott, Abbey Road Studios, 7 December 1989. *Standing, left to right*: Mark Germino, Chris Rea, Max Middleton, Nick Lowe, Dave Edmunds, Mark Knopfler, and Guy Fletcher. *Seated*: Alan Freeman, Cliff Richard. (*Jamie Scott*).

being given the 10.00 p.m. to midnight slot. The ever-invincible John Walters persuaded a reluctant Derek Chinnery that Peel's show, the most demanding and innovative in their schedule, should not be interfered with. Moreover, he would probably be playing records to an audience of adolescents before the watershed—records by groups with near-the-knuckle names like 'The Slits', 'The Molesters', and 'The Vibrators'. The prospect that Radio 1 might thus corrupt the minds of young listeners meant that John Peel would keep his late-night show for four nights a week. Nevertheless, Tommy was given the corresponding slot on Friday. Much as he admired and respected Tommy as a fellow DJ, John was furious at airtime apparently being taken from the young new outfits he was anxious to give a chance; instead, this airtime would be returned to rock dinosaurs.[9] In time, John took some consolation from the fact that Tommy was also keen to focus on young new bands (albeit from the hard rock genre rather than the alternative music scene). He was also glad that Tommy, like Alan Freeman, was equally happy to play punk as well as NWOBHM (New Wave of British Heavy Metal).

For the first few years, *The Friday Rock Show* was the only nationally available outlet for such music, and Tommy's obvious enthusiasm for giving a platform to new bands and his rapport with fans made it an instant favourite with regular listeners. The show also included a regular competition, 'The Friday Night Connection', introduced to the sound of Van der Graaf Generator's version of 'Theme One', an instrumental written for Radio 1 by Beatles producer George Martin in 1967. Added to this were studio sessions, live performances, and sometimes recordings from the BBC radio archives, live and vintage sessions from Led Zeppelin, Jethro Tull, Uriah Heep, The Nice, Genesis, and others. Interspersed throughout the programme were jingles written and performed by Samson and Vow Wow, plus incidental music from The Mahavishnu Orchestra, John Mayall & The Bluesbreakers, Santana, Stanley Clarke, and others.

One result of Tommy's appearance was that he was now the standard bearer for airing not only heavy rock, but also progressive music. Until the summer of 1978, John Peel had been playing new releases by Yes, Boston, and Emerson, Lake and Palmer. Any enthusiasm he had once had for these groups had long since waned with what he described as 'a disgraceful display of truculence' as part of his review function. Now, even though John had lost his Friday-night show, he had *carte blanche* to play exactly what he liked. It was some compensation for losing one evening of his weekly airtime. Although he vented his indignation on air and in the press, Tommy knew his colleague well enough to take it on the chin, as he commented about four months into his show. No matter what disparaging things 'Peely' might have said on air with regards to the

Friday-night listenership ('He thinks you're all balding and got false teeth,' Tommy said), it should be remembered that John had long been at the forefront of great music, and he was always ready to defend Tommy from ill-informed criticism.

Tommy was an unashamed fan of John; 'I like what he plays,' he remarked. 'I like his idealism.' Both men had much in common in addition to being presenters who were more interested in the music they played than the cult of personality. They were the only Radio 1 DJs who had served in the forces—Tommy in the Merchant Navy, John in the RAF—having both left England to work in US radio and traded on non-existent Beatles connections to get their jobs, then returning home. They both presented programmes for the British Forces Broadcasting Service, and they shared some musical common ground. As the mainstays of the station's night-time broadcasting during the week, they maintained a healthy mutual respect, always endorsing each other as music lovers who never tired of seeking out new acts within their genres. For them, it often seemed like a full-time job receiving and trying to listen to all the demos sent in by aspiring, hopeful young artists, eager for their moment of glory on air if not for a record contract.

By the end of the 1970s, the music weeklies were gradually attracting different audiences, aided by their healthy circulations. *New Musical Express* was the darling of John Peel's audience with its coverage of punk and reggae as well as a degree of alternative politics. *Melody Maker* still gave coverage to folk and jazz as well as catering for a readership more interested in rock, progressive, soul, and reggae, as did *Sounds*, which was more identified than any other title with NWOBHM and seen as more in tune with Vance's most faithful listeners. The other two music papers, *Record Mirror* and *Disc and Music Echo*, continued to compete for a more pop, chart-orientated audience.

Nevertheless, heavy rock was increasingly identified as lacking in political correctness. This was nothing new in popular music; The Rolling Stones had led the way many years before, with lyrics and album covers that often strayed into blatant if tongue-in-cheek misogyny. Several Stones songs sailed close to the wind—'Brown Sugar' featured the line 'Hear him whip the women just around midnight'—but they were rarely off the airwaves after being released, and they were never threatened with an outright ban or confined to post-watershed evening airtime. Songs by Led Zeppelin, AC/DC, and Rainbow were also criticised on similar grounds, and Tommy sometimes had to defend the genre against taunts of sexism. What, asked interviewer Dave McCullough, if he was to find himself playing 'a fiercely red-blooded over-the-top' HM track? Tommy assured him that if he came across a song that indicated or related to rape, or condoned violence against women, he would not play it.[10] However, hard rock was not the only genre with lyrical minefields for the unwary DJ. Two years earlier, on his reggae show, Tommy had played a number by Linton Kwesi Johnson about the Special Patrol Group when it was under *sub judice*; he regretted it afterwards.

In November 1979, on the Friday show's first anniversary, a Top 10 of listeners' favourite tracks was broadcast. 'Now We Are One' ('Two', 'Three', and so on in succeeding years) never achieved the iconic status of John Peel's 'Festive Fifty', but it still provided an interesting barometer of all-time greats within the genre. The fact that five records from the Peel 1976 list appeared in Tommy Vance's Top 10 (Pink Floyd's 'Shine on You Crazy Diamond', Derek and the Dominoes' 'Layla', Lynyrd Skynyrd's 'Freebird', Deep Purple's 'Child in Time', and, naturally, Led Zeppelin's 'Stairway to Heaven' at No. 1) was evidence that many listeners had partially switched allegiance from one programme to the other.

Tommy was unashamedly a music lover. 'I'm not funny, I'm not pretty,' he once said. 'My whole reason for existence is that I'm a disc jockey. My interest is in the music.' The technical staff who worked with him on the show always loved the experience, partly as it was extremely loud. As it went out late at night the Radio 3 and Radio 4 studios were sufficiently far away for no one to complain, everyone could turn up the speakers and rock out. They were aware that Tommy knew a great deal about the music; he loved and respected the genre and the artists who made it, and he really used to crank it out to the max. It was a real experience being in a studio with him, seeing how he worked with other people. All the major rock bands adored him, and to them he was an absolute god.

His fellow jocks likewise had the greatest respect for him. According to Dave Cash, who had known him at Capital Radio, he was a very private man, but always reliable, a total professional, and above all 'part of the group that actually cared about the music [they were] playing'. Once Tommy was in the studio and on air, he said, he was in Valhalla:

> I just love this stuff. It's better than anything else I've ever had in my life as a stimulant. Music is the best buzz in the world for me. Unfortunately, when you turn all the speakers up, what happens is the sound waves radiate all over the studio and things actually move within it, and I'll never forget—because it was like a suicidal number—I was watching a jingle cartridge in resonance to the music it was playing at such a hell of a volume in the studio—I just watched it move right across a set of shelves and then deliberately fall right on to the turntable and smash the record that I was playing on the air. I knew what was happening—I could see it happening—but I was so enraptured by the music that I didn't want it to stop![11]

As a DJ who was not only passionate about the music he loved but who also scrupulously researched everything he played on air, he was unerringly well-informed. Modestly, he said that in no way did he set himself up as a fount of knowledge in any field, always insisting that he was not an expert, but an enthusiast. Listeners might have disagreed, particularly after hearing him on his regular appearances as a guest reviewer of new releases on Radio 1's *Round Table* on Friday afternoons. There, his comments on each record were unfailingly as informative (if not more so) than any of his daytime colleagues. It gave him enormous satisfaction to be a radio presenter, but he stressed that he was essentially a communicator, not a headbanger. He remarked, '... I'm not headbanging because it hurts my head!' At this time, he almost gave the impression that he thrived on the insecurity of his work as a DJ. By the early 1980s, he admitted that he was enjoying himself even more than he did at the start of his career:

> ... [It is] more of a challenge the longer you keep going. The challenge is to stay in the race. There's always somebody in the wings ... The competition aspect is good. I find it gives you the edge.[12]

For him, there was no room for complacency.

Each week, the Friday night programme received a massive postbag, much of it requesting songs and asking for information about the music played. Sometimes answering the latter might take a couple of hours, and it was not unusual for him to be three months or more behind with the backlog. Questions such as 'That show back in 1973 and what was that Pink Fairies track you played on it?' invariably meant some trawling through archives from the pre-internet age. A devoted listener rang in one evening to make a request and was astonished when Tommy himself picked up the phone. He roared with laughter at his fan's speechlessness; 'You weren't expecting me to answer, then!'

There were also inevitably many demo tapes received from young hopefuls. Tommy called it 'murder', because two hours a week meant they were tight on time, and the chances of being able to broadcast any of these hopefuls on air were slim. 'It's sad,' he admitted, 'and I know it'll sound maudlin and over-emotional but I really do care about the stuff we don't play. Who knows? Maybe those people deserve a break.'[13]

His unerring enthusiasm proved infectious to listeners. Writing in *Sounds*, Dave McCullough praised the show's 'no frills, utterly competent, brilliantly understated, genuinely warm charisma'. He continued:

> [It brings sense to] an otherwise nonsensical Heavy Metal game. It makes

HM into something like a Ghost Train at a fair. Fun! Frightening! Dark and Dank! And you come out at the end unharmed![14]

The 'voice on legs' was ever in demand for voiceovers, whether they were needed for a station ID—'1FM'—a trailer for another programme, a new jingle, a public service announcement about AIDS, or even a TV commercial for the other side. Like Simon Bates, one of the regular Radio 1 daytime presenters, he had a great bass-baritone voice with brilliant projection, and with his experience at the microphone, he would do everything in one take.

Although he was identified mainly with the hard rock and heavy metal genre, in May 1980 Tommy joined the regular team of presenters on *Top of the Pops* for four and a half years. As a long-time fan of The Who, he was particularly pleased one Thursday evening in August 1980 to have Roger Daltrey as a celebrity co-host, even if the latter expressed some displeasure at having made a special effort to be there on the understanding that The Clash would be featured, only to find out that they were not on the programme after all. Roger may or may not have been aware that The Clash were one of the few punk groups who refused to appear on the show, although they could hardly exercise a right of veto over their singles being featured while they were in the charts. 'Do you like disco, Roger?' Vance asked at one point.

'Oh, I hate it,' was the terse reply. Unfortunately for him, a film clip for Village People's 'Can't Stop the Music'—an ironic title, considering the context—was coming up next.

About six months later, Tommy was asked if he would always be a DJ. He replied that he knew no other way of earning a living—notwithstanding the fact that most of his income was from 'being a commercial voice' and doing voiceovers for a large number of adverts. At the time, he revealed that he made £80 for the show on Friday nights 'and not much more' for *Top of the Pops*. Did the mock-voice that he used on his commercials, it was suggested, not seep over into the music jockeying as well? He conceded that the interviewer had a point:

> I think at times there is an element of falsification, of projecting image, but that can be after you've had a really bad day and you've STILL to go on at 10.00 at night. I HOPE it's no more than ten per cent at the most at any given time.[15]

However, Tommy's tastes always remained unashamedly eclectic, whether it was quality pop, reggae, punk, or even disco. 'I like anything,' he often said, 'as long as it's good!' In the summer of 1980, he also took over the

Saturday afternoon music magazine show *Rock On* for several months, which featured new releases and interviews with big names. Radio 1, he said, was thriving:

> Obviously no garden is completely rosy but I think it's well and solidly in bloom. The feeling there is positive and adventurous and good. And that is NOT bullshit. You get it as soon as you walk through the front doors. You genuinely get a buzz. I nearly got into a fight the other night, I was a fraction away from it, I was a bit smashed at the time, when somebody I was having dinner with started to have a go at the Radio 1 producers. I KNOW the amount of effort those guys are putting into programmes.[16]

In January 1982, Tommy took over from Tony Blackburn as presenter of the Top 40 chart show on Radio 1 every Sunday afternoon. Although musically this might have been the polar opposite to his Friday evening programme, he approached it and the necessary fact-finding with the same professionalism and meticulous standards. He was, in a sense, coming back to his roots, as he had started his career in Top 40 radio in America. The discipline with which he had been schooled—namely having just ten seconds to say what he needed to say before playing the record—proved invaluable once again. It was similar to his role when compering *Top of the Pops*, when he generally prefaced his introduction to each performance or video with a few informative words about the artist. The old 'this is … that was' routine was 'boring':

> What I tried to do in that ten-second break was to try and impart some sort of information. I would spend eight hours on the phone to all the record companies, researching every single record in the Top 40, to find out where the artist comes from, find out anything about the songwriters, particularly the producers, maybe the type of instrumentation that was used on the record, and really research what it was all about—and then translate that knowledge that I had accrued into something I could say in ten seconds. I really enjoyed doing it because it was a challenge.[17]

At the end of each chart show, he would sign off with the words 'Ain't music great!' None of his listeners could ever doubt that it was sincerely meant. His stewardship of the chart and the countdown came to an end on New Year's Day 1984, when he handed over to Simon Bates. However, in the autumn of that same year, he was given an additional evening show on Radio 1. Much to the chagrin of John Peel—now cut back to only three evenings a week—for the next year or so, Tommy filled in the 10.00 p.m. to 12 midnight slot on Thursday with *Into The Music*, a more eclectic selection of album-oriented rock (AOR), which allowed him to present a choice ranging from The Beatles, Bad Company, and Bryan Adams to Dire Straits, Meat Loaf, and Billy Ocean. Although John was annoyed to be losing a second evening of broadcasting, he and Tommy continued to enjoy a good working relationship. By now David Jensen had left the BBC, so Tommy and John were occasional joint co-presenters on *Top of the Pops*. John saw a kindred spirit in Tommy; they both cared more about the music than the trappings of radio celebrity.

At the same time, Tommy was also interviewing various celebrities for the BBC World Service, from the Prince of Wales to Mick Jagger. He and a couple of partners also opened two commercial recording studios—Silk Sound and The Bridge—in central London, producing radio and television commercials for BP, Shell, Gillette, and other companies. From 1988, he was in the presenter's chair for a daily drive-time slot on Greater London Radio, and from time to time he appeared as master of ceremonies at award shows, concerts, and festivals. When he appeared onstage as a compere at the annual Monsters of Rock show at Castle Donington between 1981 and 1986, fans good-naturedly pelted him with bottles that were occasionally filled with urine. Some groups resented this practice, angrily telling the audience to stop before people got hurt. Fortunately, Tommy had seen fit to wear a protective American football helmet. Tommy's involvement came to an end after six festivals, after he had complained in the music press that the DJ equipment he had been supplied with in between sets was faulty. He was not invited back.

The *Friday Rock Show* always remained the programme with which he was most associated. AC/DC's 'Rock 'n' Roll Damnation' had been the opening record on the first show, and in December 1981 he recorded a festive special with the group which went out on Christmas Day. Tommy helped to break new ground one week in 1983, when his programme was the first to be broadcast solely using CDs.

Deep Purple were another group who appreciated his support. They had disbanded in 1976, its members finding success with the offshoot groups Rainbow, Whitesnake, and Gillan. When the latter were signed to Virgin Records in 1980 and their album *Glory Road* entered the charts at No. 3, Richard Branson threw a curry party for the group and friends at Hammersmith, with Tommy among the special guests. In April 1984, Tommy broke the news on his show that following months of speculation, the classic early 1970s Purple line-up was about to reform. That autumn, shortly after the release of their comeback album *Perfect Strangers* and while they were rehearsing for a tour, Tommy interviewed all five members in depth for a feature that was broadcast on his show in November.

Without his support, the NWOBHM would almost certainly never have become the major force in the early 1980s that it did, as many of its leading lights have readily acknowledged. On the title track of Saxon's fourth album, *Denim and Leather*, released in the autumn of 1981, the band paid tribute to Tommy's programme with the line 'Did you listen to the radio every Friday night?' Joe Elliott, lead vocalist of Def Leppard—one of the groups who, in their early days, had benefited most from exposure on the Friday night slot—was unstinting in his praise. He pointed out that there had long been local stations that had had their own rock show, but Tommy's was the only one on national radio. Listeners might hear the occasional track on daytime radio—such as Golden Earring's 'Radar Love'—but this was rare:

> So when you tuned in to listen to Tommy, you knew you were in for an education. You listened to the show, and he mixed in unknown, unsigned bands like us with the more established artists. When NWOBHM happened, he would play us, Iron Maiden and so many others. It was the only place where you could hear young rock and metal bands on air.

It was not only Vance's championship of and unrestrained enthusiasm for rock music that appealed to Elliott. He continued:

> What I loved about Tommy was that he never slagged anybody off. Even off the record, he was always positive about everyone.

It was a refreshing attitude that he rarely found in anybody else in the profession.[18]

More established groups were equally appreciative of what Tommy was doing for them on air. When Deep Purple produced a programme for their Knebworth appearance in 1985, it noted cryptically inside: 'There's only one national rock show in Britain, tucked away where the powers that be think it will do least harm'.

Tommy's technical staff also thoroughly relished the Tommy Vance experience. Some years later, Mike Woolmans, a technical operator who worked closely with him for several years, recalled putting together a Radio 1 documentary on Judas Priest, *Between the Hammer and the Anvil*, and had a great time devising audio tricks, tape loop edits, motorbike effects, and sounds played backwards, all in the pre-sampling days. The programme won a Sony Award.

The BBC launched Greater London Radio in 1988, with Tommy hosting the afternoon drive-time show—a blend of 'rock and rolling news'. He was also part of the launch team for Virgin Radio and presented rock videos on VH1. By the end of the decade, Britain had a far wider choice of television and radio channels. The hard rock and heavy metal that Tommy had flown the flag for so well was now more accessible, and his show was arguably less important and less unique than before. Moreover, since the return of Alan Freeman, there were now two weekly helpings on Radio 1 catering for the same audience.

If the shape of British broadcasting was gradually changing, so was rock music itself. In 1978, the music featured by Tommy Vance and John Peel on their respective shows was very different. Fifteen years later, it was converging. Mainstream rock was no longer strictly the preserve of the NWOBHM or long-established classic groups like Deep Purple and Black Sabbath, who had disbanded and regrouped with odd changes in personnel. Now the mainstream was embracing names such as the Manic Street Preachers, Faith No More, and Nirvana, including contemporary movements like grunge. Some acts were crossing over and almost equally at home on both shows. During Tommy's final year, John Peel was again broadcasting on Friday nights for three hours from 11.00 p.m., with Tommy in the preceding slot. He was increasingly playing groups originally aired on John's show, and during their penultimate handover on 26 March, Tommy's final record was from Dinosaur Jr. 'How nice to see so many of my bands creeping into your programme,' John told him on air. 'Perhaps it'll be the turn of The Fall fairly soon. I look forward to that.'

Tommy always retained fond memories of working for the Corporation. He later recalled:

> [The most gratifying experience was] going down and sitting in a BBC studio representing the BBC because nobody does it better and it will be, as far as I can visualise between now and the end of the century, the only place where you will get creative radio whereby they will take chances. Nobody else is taking chances. It's homogenised, statisticised and all worked out and nobody in commercial radio, or the commercial radio that I'm involved in, talks about music, none of them.[19]

When Tommy announced in 1993 that he was going to leave Radio 1, the technical staff who worked with him were amazed. However, there was method in his madness; he had just been promised a regular drive-time show on Virgin, playing classic, adult-orientated rock. It was his dream gig. As a replacement on the *Friday Rock Show*, the BBC chose Claire Sturgess, who had previously worked as a radio production assistant on the Simon Bates mid-morning show and had presented *The Evening Session* for a week. Simon and Tommy had both been very supportive of her, and the latter endorsed her unequivocally as his successor, inviting her to sit in and co-present on the final two evening shows. This, she said, was typical of the generosity of the man, and she had 'a whale of a time' with him. Almost anybody else of that stature who was doing their final show would not have wanted to share the honours with anybody else.

Tommy completed his final show on 2 April 1993, closing with AC/DC's 'Rock 'n' Roll Damnation', with which he had opened his first show some fourteen years earlier. It was the end of an era. The fresh Virgin Radio line-up he was joining included fellow Radio 1 expatriates such as Richard Skinner (Joint Programming Controller and Head of Music) and Emperor Rosko. Even so, it must have seemed something of an anti-climax after his fifteen glorious years at Radio 1. The station initially followed an adventurous musical policy, with Tommy allowed some personal input over tracks, but it did not last for long before the dreaded ad-driven playlist became mandatory. Tommy soon expressed regret over having left Radio 1, although it is unclear whether he, like John Peel, would have survived Matthew Bannister's purge of the elder, more experienced presenters in 1993. He later damned Virgin with faint praise:

> [It is a package that is] doing absolutely nothing which is new in the radio marketplace whatsoever, and I think they would be the first to admit it ... what you have is a complete clone of any major station in Los Angeles, New York, Johannesburg or Sydney. It's doing nothing other than running a system and it's not for me.[20]

He soon found a more congenial home, being given a chance to revive the *Friday Rock Show* for the digital channel VH1 and on the DAB and internet offshoot Virgin Classic Rock. He remained interested in new musical trends throughout the years, often stating his opinion that the best album of all time had not yet been recorded.

Now in his mid-fifties, he was perhaps content to convey the impression that he was simply a hack, a voiceover man, a larynx on legs, content to sell whatever was in the script. He still had one of the most inimitable voices in broadcasting history, one with which he could sell almost anything. His love of music and broadcasting had never abated. If, as some of those close to him suspected, he had been considering semi-retirement in Spain after three decades or so as a presenter, he had a change of heart and he was soon back in his usual role, playing music once more on the Costa del Sol's Spectrum FM.

Although his new work meant he would never be in front of a national audience again, arguably never quite measuring up to his past achievements, his voice remained very much in demand. In 2003, he could be heard providing the narration for a series on Channel 5, *Dumber and Dumber*, based around clips of people caught on camera doing ridiculous things. As ever, he approached it with his customary professionalism, but to music fans it was surely a waste of his talent. At least he was able to put in an appearance on the comedic music quiz *Never Mind the Buzzcocks*, on which he correctly identified Pete Langford and 'Butch' Baker of The Barron Knights, alongside four interlopers, on a question of 'spot the real member'.

A less happy and briefer excursion onto the small screen came a year later, when he was a contestant in the ITV reality show *Hell's Kitchen*. As someone who had formerly worked in the Merchant Navy catering division, he was well-qualified to join, but he stayed there for only twenty-four hours. He and another recent recruit, athlete Dwain Chambers, resented being constantly on the receiving end of abuse from chef and presenter Gordon Ramsay. Moreover, according to his agent, Jon Roseman, Tommy thought the show was dangerous. He was very tired at the time and felt the kitchen was an unsafe environment to be in, full of boiling water, fire, and fat; he had only narrowly escaped a scalding. In short, he left to save his own finger and somebody else's.

The expanding multi-channel television market might have seemed the only place for him to go in the twenty-first century. Having been interviewed in 1998 about the current state of British radio, he said that he felt it had gone backwards in many ways. For him, there was a place for a more creative, freeform radio that he thought 'would be greater appreciated by the public in this country, but maybe not by the bankers who put up the money'.

Nevertheless, there were always new outlets to be found. Interviewed in February 2005, Tommy talked enthusiastically of starting to work with Spectrum FM, a Spanish-based station that provided a mix of 1980s, 1990s, and current chart music for an English-speaking audience. He had been to Spain and undertaken some initial work for the station a couple of years beforehand, 'trying to set up various things', but for personal reasons he needed to return to Britain for a while. During that time, he had been recording his shows in London and sending them to Spain for transmission. Although his work was still based in the capital, he was now planning to find himself an apartment somewhere in Spain as he was very fond of the country—the culture, the tempo, and the climate—and especially the beer. His Spectrum show, he promised, would be the same format as his fondly-remembered Radio 1 show—'a two-hour blast of rock'. He admitted, '[It was] not so much my music of choice but definitely what I'm known for. I've done it so long that people almost associate me with rock.'[21]

That was a masterly understatement, a preface to what might have been a whole new beginning. Moreover, perhaps the change came at the right time; with hindsight, his closest personal friend, 'Softly'—a former member of staff at A & M Records—said that Tommy was stressed, feared that he might be finished, and was working hard to rebuild his career. Like others before him, he had discovered that the career of a radio presenter was an insecure one, and anything but a job for life. Some twenty years earlier, he had said that the challenge was 'to stay in the race', but having dropped out of it, he realised that getting back in was easier said than done, particularly at his time of life.

Sadly, it would not be long before the unmistakable voice of the Music Vendor would be silenced for good. Within a week of being interviewed about his plans in Spain, Tommy suffered a stroke while driving back to his flat after hosting the *Friday Rock Show* on VH1. He was admitted to Darent Valley Hospital near Dartford, Kent, and three days later, early on 6 March 2005, he passed away. In the words of Softly, 'he went out like a firework'. Despite being very different presenters, John Peel and Tommy Vance had dominated most of the evening output at Radio 1 for several years, and both were respected as giants in their field. It is ironic that both died within less than five months of each other, and both at almost exactly the same age.

Friends, family, and colleagues gathered at Golders Green Crematorium on 15 March to pay their respects and say farewell. The ceremony was organised by 'Softly', whose real name was Jon Adrian. Among those who attended were Tommy's estranged wife 'Cookie' (Stella) and daughter, Jessie, and his friends and colleagues from the radio, including Paul Gambaccini, Richard Skinner, Adrian Juste, Simon Bates, Duncan Johnson, Dave Cash, and a sadly ailing Alan Freeman. Also present were studio staff and backstage people from the various stations at which Tommy had worked, Deep Purple members Ian Gillan and Jon Lord, and actor Robert Lindsay, who was married at the time to Tommy's former partner, actress Diana Weston. At Tommy's request, the event was turned into a celebration of his life. While everyone felt sadness at their loss, it turned into a parade of people telling stories about him and the kind of person he was. As he had once said, 'When you're gone, you're gone. I don't want anybody weeping for me.'[22] Softly said that he hated black ties and did not want anyone wearing them at the funeral. Unfortunately, many people there were unaware of this and arrived sporting one all the same.

Several affectionate, moving, and yet lively addresses were given, and Diana Weston read John Masefield's 'Sea Fever' in memory of Tommy's days at sea. One particular moment that stood in the memory of everybody present was when Softly, addressing the crowd, told them that he had been with Tommy and Cookie at the hospital when he died. Later that day, or perhaps on the next, the question of organ donation came up. No one knew what Tommy's views on the subject had been, so they agreed to let the doctors run a few tests on his body and take it from there. A few hours later, the nurse reappeared to say that they were terribly sorry but there was no question of using anything—Tommy was 'completely used up—buggered!' At this, everyone fell about in uncontrollable laughter. It was an epitaph that Tommy would surely have relished to the full.

In the words of Jon Myer, who had been Tommy's producer at Greater London Radio, he was 'a lovely man and a joy to work with' and 'had the most rock 'n' roll funeral [he had] ever attended!' There was a notable absence of religion, and the music included George Martin's 'Theme One', Pink Floyd's 'Comfortably Numb', and Neil Young's 'Like a Hurricane'. It all finished with a recording of the end of one of Tommy's rock shows and the strains of AC/DC, after which the guests then trooped off to raise a glass or two to him at the nearest hostelry.

A tribute night was held at the Royal Albert Hall on 31 March 2006, just over a year later, headlined by Judas Priest and supported by Ian Gillan and Friends and The Scorpions. Tommy Vance's spirit would surely have been looking down with approval.

5
Roger Scott

The other four disc jockeys in this book all had the good fortune to live into their sixties and beyond, and three were still broadcasting regularly less than a month before their deaths. The fifth was still in harness at the time of his final illness, but he hung up his headphones and switched off his microphone all too soon. At an age when most of his colleagues were in their prime and had many more years to look forward to, Roger Scott was gone. For most of his career in Britain, he had been broadcasting to a small section of the nation, but he was widely acclaimed as the best DJ that commercial radio had had to offer. A little more than a year after he joined Radio 1 and became a major national broadcasting name, he was dead.

Roger Scott was born in Barnet on 23 October 1943 and educated at Surbiton Grammar School. For him, the discovery of the joys of radio came through listening to comedy and drama, particularly the former. *The Goon Show*, *Hancock's Half-Hour*, *Ray's a Laugh*, *Beyond Our Ken*, and *Round the Horne* meant that on Sunday afternoons, there was only one activity. As for the drama titles, *Dick Barton's Special Agent* and *Journey into Space* were both musts; however, when he later heard a re-run of one of the episodes, he felt that it had not aged well and that it now sounded 'diabolical'.

In 1958, through the medium of television, Roger was introduced to rock 'n' roll. A glimpse on a little 6-inch screen of '*Oh Boy!*' and, more importantly, Cliff Richard performing 'Move It', and he was hooked. The latter was the first single he ever bought.

Roger then discovered Radio Luxembourg, and particularly *The Teen and Twenty Disc Club*. With so little pop and rock 'n' roll on the BBC Light Programme at the time, gathering around a radio to listen to Radio Luxembourg, even though the reception was poor, was an essential shared experience for Roger and everyone else in his age group. From Cliff he graduated to Elvis Presley, acquiring an extensive collection of the latter's singles as well. The latest by the Everly Brothers, Buddy Holly, and others soon followed. In his teens, Roger began playing records out of the window of his home in London, watching the reaction of passers-by to the music.

When he took his GCEs in 1960, he had no idea what he wanted to do for a career. He thought of joining the Royal Air Force and becoming a helicopter pilot with the Fleet Air Arm, but he did not have enough O-levels. After seeing an advertisement for the Merchant Navy, he applied and was accepted at the interview stage. He joined as a navigating apprentice and became a deck officer, spending thirteen months sailing around the world a couple of times. He later reflected on the experience, stating, '... goodness me, did I grow up.' No less importantly, he was introduced to a totally different kind of broadcasting on his travels. At sea, he said, radio was the most vital piece of equipment of all:

> ... your only contact with the outside world, the World Service, the Merchant Navy programme—you had to hear that. It was hearing all the other things coming in from America, as you go over there around the coast of America or to the American Forces network coming out of Vietnam at the time, or from Japan and just totally different and totally alien to anything I had ever heard before, and so exciting. Jumping ahead to 1964, we were travelling in an iron ore carrier from Chile to Japan, backwards and forwards, backwards and forwards, mind-numbing—but the only good thing about it was you passed really close to Hawaii. You never stopped there but you listened to the radio in Hawaii, and you'd know exactly where you were going to be on the chart when you could first hear the radio stations there.[1]

The station that enthused him particularly at this point was Hawaii KORL. Partly out of curiosity and partly because there was little else to do, one day he sat down and wrote to the owner of the station to ask for more information.

> What were these jingles, these commercials and these DJs? I mean, where do they all come from, how does it all work? And the bloke actually wrote back to me, sent a very detailed letter explaining it all. I wrote to him again—I never met him—but this correspondence continued as we went backwards and forward across the Pacific, and I really got intrigued.[2]

In time, these letters would prove an invaluable education to the aspiring young broadcaster. Meanwhile, in 1965 he took his final exams after his apprenticeship and got a second mate's ticket, going out on a brand-new oil tanker. Despite his progress, at around this point he decided that the Merchant Navy was not the life for him. He found it increasingly boring and could not visualise doing it forever. One thing he found unpalatable was the continual drunkenness; 'I've seen brains disintegrating,' he said, 'pink elephants walking the deck.'[3] By the end of the year, he was home on leave.

Next he read an article in *The Sunday Times* about how the local radio association was lobbying parliament to introduce legal commercial radio in Britain. This, he knew, would happen sooner or later, and when it did, he was aware that there must be very few people in Britain who would know how it worked or how to run it properly. He had two options from which to choose—either stay with the Merchant Navy, or take a giant leap into the unknown and give broadcasting a try. Having been paid off after his trips around the high seas and with a respectable sum of money in the bank, he bought a one-way ticket to America. Like Tommy Vance, Roger thought that there was only one place to go and live the dream for any aspiring radio DJ; even if he was unable to find a paid job, he would reap the benefits of work experience.

Making his way to Albany, New York, in the bleak midwinter, he turned up at the front door of Station WPTR. The station was noted for its very powerful signal, which could be picked up a long distance away—even to the south of Ireland. It was an inhospitable night; there was a howling blizzard, and the station was in the middle of a field. A member of the opened the door to Roger and suggested that he might like to go and spend the night in a motel, returning the next day. When he came back, he asked for a job, assuring them that he was anxious to learn how radio had worked and that he was prepared to do anything—even cleaning the ashtrays. As luck would have it, they had just aired a Beatles special, and they needed somebody English to take part in a promotion in which they would give away a jukebox. To him fell the very pleasant job of pretending he was a friend of The Beatles, The Rolling Stones, Herman's Hermits, The Swinging Blue Jeans, and The Dave Clark Five—some of the British acts who had become really big stateside. 'You can go on air and say you know them all,' he was told.

Happy to oblige, he acted out the little white lie convincingly, and the station was besieged with calls to ask who this English guy was. As John Peel and Tommy Vance had discovered, it helped young Brits to pretend to know The Beatles if they wanted to work as DJs in American radio. Towards the end, Roger admitted that his whole life had been a 'con', beginning with the days that he had talked himself onto the American airwaves as a Beatles' expert and personal friend of the group (a pattern is evidently emerging here). He was accordingly asked to stay on, so he took out a work permit. On 1 April 1966, he started his own show, kicking off with The Dave Clark Five's 'Try Too Hard', a single that had flopped in Britain but made the American Top 20.

Once he had started, he knew he had found his true vocation:

> I'd never given it a thought doing this, but once I'd started it, it felt so right, it was just this opportunity to do all those things you'd been told not to do, like playing records loud, playing rock 'n' roll records loud so that not only could the neighbours hear but people in Greenland as well. I had the loudest record player going, this 50,000-watt throbbing transmitter out at the back of this studio and these huge towers, and I'm sitting there with the world's loudest record player—and being encouraged to do it—and being paid to do it! This was crazy, but it didn't take me long to decide that this was the life and if I could keep doing this for a few years without getting found out then that's fine.[4]

He would later say that 1966 was the most exciting year of his life. On a personal level, it was the year he began work as a DJ, taking to it as naturally as a duck to water. In terms of musical history, it was the year that The Beatles played their last live concerts (apart from their impromptu rooftop session in Central London during their last months together). When they undertook their final tour in America that summer, Roger went to see them at Suffolk Downs Racetrack, Boston, with two busloads of fans. With his ID, the stewards allowed him and his tape recorder to the front until he was within 12 feet of the stage. The Beatles' performance and amplifiers were all but drowned out by the sound of screaming fans, so it was doubtful that he would have taken away the audio souvenir he was after. His abiding memory of the occasion was of George Harrison, who had noticed the recorder, giving him a dirty look all the way through the set.

Throughout this time, Roger was listening to other presenters and steadily learning his craft. As he observed his peers and their different styles, copying each of them in some small way, he arrived at a style that 'boiled down into something that wasn't any of them', eventually developing a unique flair. Everybody, he said, went through that when they wanted to be a DJ:

> The secret is to go through that and come out of it at the other end, having discovered yourself and that you are this unique person, and you don't have to sound like anybody else. You can just be yourself, you don't have to hide behind some other identity that you're stealing. Again in my case, it just comes down to that's me, and what I do on the radio is what I am, and it's not me adopting any sort of fake persona.[5]

One of his peers at WPTR, Larry Dean (whose real name was Frank Laseter), told Roger he was to join a pirate ship in the North Sea and broadcast on Radio England. The night before he went, Roger discovered him making copies of a jingle package that had just been purchased for the station, including all the jingles for the jocks working there. As a result, when Larry arrived at his new station, everyone else who was broadcasting there would have to use one of the names in the package instead of their own. Thus a simple case of DJ identity theft came about. Roger was perhaps an exception to the frequent rule of DJs using an alias; throughout his career, he nearly always worked under his real name. It is therefore ironic that he later discovered there was a *faux* Roger Scott broadcasting several thousand miles away. When listeners told him admiringly that they remembered hearing him on the pirates, he admitted with a smile that the Roger Scott they were referring to was not actually him. There was another British presenter, Greg Bance, who worked as a television continuity announcer as well as a DJ; he called himself 'Roger Scott' on Radio Essex, Radio 270, and, for its last few days on air, Radio Caroline North. He was presumably a Pink Floyd fan as he was later on Radio Northsea International as 'Arnold Layne'. That makes two Roger Scotts at least.

The original Roger Scott was also moving on. He loaded everything into the back of his Mustang convertible and went up to Montreal, where he had been invited to join 1470 CFOX, a small country-music station that was in the process of altering its format to one based around the Top 40. Canada was the place to be, especially as he desperately wanted to be in Montreal in 1967 to experience the world convening at Expo '67. This was the 1967 International and Universal Exposition, which celebrated Canada's centenary; it would be staged for six months throughout the coming year.

It was fortunate that he was still in love with his giant record player, for now he would be conducting his love affair with the decks in a punishing schedule. His brief was to run a show on his own for thirty-six hours per week, from 8.00 p.m. to 2.00 a.m. every Monday to Friday and 12.00 p.m. to 6.00 p.m. on Sunday. His first contract was worth $600 Canadian, equivalent to about £300 in 1967 prices. That was the schedule in theory. In practice, shortly before he reached the end of his shift at 2.00 a.m., he would ask if anybody was still up and, if so, if they wanted him to stay on. Almost at once, the switchboard would light up with eager night-owl listeners hanging on to his every word (or record), pleading with him to keep going. Although the station was supposed to close down at 2.00 a.m. for four hours, Roger, a glutton for punishment if ever there was one, found himself carrying on frequently for the next four hours, until the breakfast show presenter came and started the broadcast day again.

In any city, there was always rivalry between the major stations. One cold and snowy morning in February 1967, Roger learned that 1470

CFOX's main competitor, 980 CKGM Montreal, had pulled some major record industry strings and was announcing a 'Canadian Exclusive First Play' of the long-awaited new Beatles release, the double-sided 'Penny Lane/Strawberry Fields Forever' single. No one else, the station assured listeners, would have access to a copy until the imminent official, collective, pan-Canadian radio launch hours later; theirs was going to be 'flown in directly from England, First Class, and retrieved from the airport by special limousine and police escort'. It would be aired on CKGM immediately upon arrival at 4.00 p.m. the next day.

Of course, Roger had secured his job at CFOX partly on the strength of his 'connection' to The Beatles, and he was more than ready for the challenge of beating his rivals at their own game. The night prior to the CKGM 'exclusive first', on his drive home, he happened to tune in to WABC 770 New York, the powerhouse American AM station, beaming in loud and clear. Almost at once, he heard both sides of the eagerly sought-after new release, a vinyl copy having been supplied to the station a few hours earlier and showcased repeatedly ever since as a WABC American Radio Premiere Exclusive. He pulled over to the first phone booth he could find, called the station's request line (long distance—in those pre-cell-phone days, this required a large quantity of coins fed into the phone booth) and was put through to Charlie Greer, the DJ who had played it, on his overnight show. Having explained his situation, Roger suggested that he was willing to leave Montreal and drive down to New York City overnight.

'Would you make me a tape copy of the two songs and drop it off to my attention at the WABC front desk before you leave the station for the day?' he asked.

'Man,' Charlie replied, 'if you're crazy enough to drive all night, all the way down and right back again for a little piece of 7" vinyl in the middle of winter, that's the least I can do for you, my friend!'

Roger set off shortly after 2.00 a.m. for New York City, a ten-hour return trip at least, to retrieve a reel-to-reel tape copy of what was the hottest musical property on the American continent—if not the world. Having negotiated the New York City morning traffic on the way in, he dashed out of WABC, precious tape in hand, and made his way back through the Manhattan chaos to the US Interstate North.

Through the perils of a sudden blinding snowstorm in upstate New York, as well as car problems near the US-Canada border, one exhausted-yet-resilient presenter finally pulled in at CFOX that same afternoon. Sprinting up the stairs and down the hallway, he barged in on-air on his startled CFOX colleague Dean Hagopian, who was in the middle of a sentence. The two giddy DJs, scarcely able to believe their luck, frantically cued up the Beatles tracks onto the tape machine live on the air. According to the studio clock, it was 3.59 p.m. and counting. One minute later, with time being of the essence, the first song on the tape, 'Strawberry Fields Forever', was on air, followed immediately by 'Penny Lane'. As the first song was playing on CFOX, Roger raced to the newsroom and set the radio to 980 CKGM to hear his competitor Buddy Gee already playing the A-side, 'Penny Lane'. Although CKGM had played the latter track first, CFOX still ended up broadcasting 'Strawberry Fields Forever' before anyone else in Canada. The result was more or less a dead heat. It was certainly not the exclusive that a stunned and rather miffed Buddy Gee and his staff, or Capitol Records, had intended it to be. Still, all's fair in love and radio war.

Roger managed to provide listeners with more excitement that summer, when he disappeared for a while. Early in July, the station broadcast a newsflash announcing that he had gone missing; he had been mysteriously 'kidnapped' and was being 'held captive' at an undisclosed location. During this 'disappearance', which lasted for several days, he was nevertheless able to deliver many live daily clues on CFOX 1470 in between the Top 40 tunes, via phone-ins at various times to the other DJs. Microphone in hand, a cup of tea in the other, and the ever-present cigarette never far away, he provided succinct bits of information and an ingenious set of clues that had to be collected in order to direct listeners to the secret hideout. The plot thickened daily as listeners scrambled around Montreal, trying to find him. His directions pointed to the man-made islands of Expo '67, where there were millions of visitors on site every week and hundreds of attractions and pavilions. Some thought it would be the Great Britain Pavilion perhaps, but others concluded that it would be too obvious.

By the sixth day of his 'disappearance', the search was at fever pitch, and groups of CFOX listeners were closing in. The elusive Roger Scott was eventually located; he had been phoning in daily from a tiny, remote broadcast booth off the beaten track, behind a clump of trees and bushes, at the back of Expo's International Youth Pavilion. The lucky listeners who ran him to earth solved the mystery to boisterous on-air cheers as he handed over a batch of Expo '67-related prizes to the delighted teens for their efforts. The proceedings closed with another headline newsflash, reporting:

> Kidnappers flee as DJ Roger Scott is found, unharmed, safe and sound by a hardy team of CFOX listeners, in a secluded back lot near the International Youth Pavilion at Expo! CFOX would like to thank all involved for their concern, support and assistance during this challenging week. Congratulations on a job well done!

Soon afterwards, Roger's career at CFOX was interrupted as a series of disagreements about musical decisions and station duties between passionate individuals had resulted in an impasse. In May 1968, he stormed off to Halifax, Nova Scotia, where station CHNS welcomed him with open arms for nine months. Enticed back by CFOX in February 1969—as cooler heads were prevailing all around—he rebounded back to Montreal, where he began to host a new underground show, *Over Under Sideways Down*, which he facetiously dubbed 'terribly revolutionary stuff'.

In the summer of 1969, Roger became friends with one of The Beatles for a short while; not only that, but he also appeared on a hit single himself. John Lennon and Yoko Ono had arrived in Montreal in May, staging an eight-day bed-in for peace in Room 1742 in The Queen Elizabeth Hotel. To mark the occasion, John asked Scott to call a long list of radio stations so they could be put on air and he could give listeners his messages of world peace around North America and the world. Without exception, they were all delighted to have the honour of broadcasting a real member of the Fab Four.

On 31 May, as the bed-in was nearing an end, John, Yoko, and the group's press officer, Derek Taylor, invited a crowd of about fifty people into the room. Among them were Tommy Smothers, Timothy Leary, Allen Ginsberg, members of the Radha Krishna Temple, Dick Gregory, Petula Clark, Roger, members of the press, and Queen Elizabeth Hotel staffers. Also present were sound engineer André Perry (in charge of the four-track tape deck) and a camera crew (who would chant along to 'Give Peace a Chance'). Roger's contribution was to beat on a coffee table in time. The Hare Krishna drumming in the hotel room and the vocals were 'sweetened' by André Perry in his studio in Montreal following transfer to eight-track, in order to mask the defects and improve the less-than-perfect hotel-room one-take recording. All this was accomplished swiftly, and the record was sent at once for mastering and pressing in Britain as John Lennon wanted it released as quickly as possible. It appeared under the name of 'Plastic Ono Band' and became a worldwide hit, although no one would have expected anything else of a single with Lennon's name attached.

Some months later, in April 1970, Roger landed an interview with Robert Plant to mark Led Zeppelin's first visit to Montreal on a North American tour. By then, Roger had come to realise that North America was never to be more than a temporary stop. As the new decade dawned, he was encouraged by news of the impending launch of legal, land-based commercial radio in Britain in the event of a new government. When the Conservatives won the general election in June 1970, this dream came a stage nearer, and he returned to the home country in late 1971. On his arrival, he discovered that such plans were still only in the early stages, and the introduction was not as advanced as he had anticipated. To pass the time, he secured a position at the United Biscuits Network, a closed-circuit station broadcasting music to all workers in the United Biscuits factories nationwide.

Early in 1973, Roger also had two separate four-week stints on BBC Radio 1. Anticipating a future in commercial radio, he presented these shows under the pseudonym of 'Bob Baker', the broadcasting handle of Robert Stoehr, a former colleague from CFOX. At this stage, he did not see himself joining the national station line-up on a regular basis. 'The BBC is a dinosaur,' he commented. 'It's like the Civil Service, and I don't like the Civil Service.'[6]

Commercial radio was given the go-ahead when the Sound Broadcasting Act was passed in 1972, giving the Independent Broadcasting Authority responsibility for organising the new Independent Local Radio stations. When an advertisement was placed for a Programme Controller at the soon-to-be-launched Capital Radio, he was the first to submit an application, and he had the honour of being chosen as the runner-up; the winning candidate was a woman from America. Soon afterwards, press reports were suggesting that the new radio station would sound rather like the old Light Programme *circa* 1958, but with advertisements—and 'not that good'. Deciding that Capital Radio was probably not going to be for him after all, he decided to return to Canada. However, then the woman who had been appointed as Controller chose not to accept the post after all, and Michael Bukht was selected instead. He immediately called Roger in for an audition (with former Radio 1 DJ Dave Cash sitting in), and Roger was promptly recruited to join the team.

London's Capital Radio went on air for the first time on 16 October 1973, with Roger filling the afternoon slot on weekdays from 4.00–6.00 p.m., later extended by one hour both ways. In its initial stages, to quote his own words, it was 'a shambles'. All they did was play records by Sergio Mendes and The Carpenters, and it seemed as if nobody was listening, with their target audience's radios remaining tuned to Radio 1 instead. Moreover, a severe British economic situation at the end of 1973 was exacerbated by the oil crisis and the three-day week. Nobody was buying advertising, and it seemed the worst possible time to launch a commercial radio station. The solution, Roger said, was to 'rock it up'—in other words, to abandon the station's easy-listening principle and rethink its music policy. From its unpromising beginnings, a more contemporary Top 40, new releases, and a choice oldies policy prevailed, and ratings improved.

Knowing exactly what sounds he wanted to share with his listeners, Roger hardly needed a producer. With his dry sense of humour and regular features, he was an undoubted asset to Capital. To him, it was all natural—a craft, a gift that was just there, and one that had been well-honed on the other side of the Atlantic. To him, there was nothing extraordinary or difficult about being on the radio.

Like Alan Freeman, whose style and love of music he always admired (and who later became a close friend), Roger Scott was renowned for his total economy of words. Listeners to both men never learned anything about their personal lives or heard either of them babbling endlessly on about their holidays or what they had been watching on TV at the weekend. They both had the essence of the great broadcaster in that they created the perfect environment for the listener to get the most out of the music. At the same time, Roger, like Alan, was a very private man as well as a consummate broadcaster, and he eschewed the personality cult beloved by others. When invited to join the Capital Radio bus and wave to the passing crowds at the Lord Mayor's parade, his reaction was a bemused, 'Who, me?' It was not his kind of thing, or as he eloquently put it, not necessarily the best use of his talents.

Similarly to John Peel, for someone who came into his own behind a microphone and could happily talk on the radio to an audience of millions, Roger was quite shy. He hated being watched while he was on the air. In the early days of Capital, the station broadcast from the Ideal Home Exhibition for some weeks. He had to do his afternoon programme in front of an audience, and he absolutely hated every moment. Colleagues and staff recalled that afterwards, on his first day back at Euston Tower, he was audibly relieved to be back 'home'. Fellow DJ Nicky Horne rounded up as many people as he could find from the production office to peer through the studio window at Roger—just to wind him up.

His passion for being on radio did not extend to television; unlike some of his contemporaries, he never saw radio as a stepping stone onto the visual medium. A brief role on the small screen, courtesy of the BBC, was an experience he never intended to repeat. In 1975 he was, as he put it, 'bullied' into taking part in *Disco!*, a TV pop quiz show that went out on Sunday afternoons during late summer and early autumn. The six-part series, shown on BBC2, was staged in various discotheques around the country and chaired by Terry Wogan, with Roger and Tim Rice (the lyricist, also a Capital presenter at that time) as team captains. Each week, a group such as 5000 Volts or Mott (formerly Mott The Hoople) would be featured playing or miming their current single. After the questions were over, the teams and their captains would join the audience, strutting their stuff on the dance floor. Roger was sure that the show irritated his bosses at Capital Radio as much as it did the BBC, and thus it pleased no one.

Perhaps it was as well that the rating figures were unspectacular and the first series remained the last. He valued his privacy too much. For a radio presenter to become public property, he said, also meant that something of the mystique and mystery of radio was destroyed. Moreover, the other staff at Capital thought that he was upset by some of the mail he received afterwards. Until then, he had been an anonymous but well-loved voice on the radio, but apparently a few viewers were disappointed to see what he actually looked like; he somehow failed to match the image they had associated with the voice. The word going around the station was that these few unpleasant letters put him off any further TV work.

For him, British pop music around 1974 was not at its best, with a preponderance of artists from the Mike Chapman and Nicky Chinn song-writing team holding sway and The Bay City Rollers outselling everybody else. A major shot in the arm for the scene arrived when Bruce Springsteen played his first British gigs in November 1975. While 'The Boss' may not have impressed John Peel unduly, Roger was greatly encouraged by the sight and sound of somebody who could still make such exciting rock 'n' roll and displayed a real commitment to the music he was performing. After seeing Bruce live, Roger played his records with such fervour and regularity that some Capital listeners complained to the Independent Broadcasting Authority and to John Whitney, the Managing Director of Capital. Scott was 'leant on', or told to reduce the amount of airplay suddenly being given to New Jersey's favourite son; however, with a little elbow room, he could get away with paying no more than lip service to such orders. Within a few years, British contemporary taste caught up with his intense admiration for the man and he was able to say, 'I told you so.' When Bruce released a live album on three CDs and five vinyl discs in 1985, Roger devoted a complete evening show to playing it from start to finish.

One of Roger's most popular slots was the 'Daily Hitline', an instant Top 10 based on listeners' votes for their current favourite record based on phone calls to the station during the preceding twenty-four hours. Towards the end of 1975, new singles such as Walker Brothers' 'No Regrets' found a place in the radio chart several weeks before they broke nationally. In June 1976, a few months after the success of 'Bohemian Rhapsody' and its parent album *A Night at the Opera*, Queen and EMI Records were reluctant to release a second single from the album. Repeated votes and a No. 1 placing in the hitline for the track 'You're My Best Friend' forced their hand, and a few weeks later it reached the national Top 10 as well. Regular listeners soon learned to tell which new release Roger wanted to go into the hitline as he would give it a spin just before the Top 10 in the hope that listeners would share his enthusiasm and vote for it the next day.

Occasionally, a complete novelty would make the Capital Hitline Chart while going totally unnoticed, perhaps even unheard, outside of London. One such record was 'Day Trip to Barnhurst', a popular item in the summer of 1980 and the only single ever released by Jackie and the Commuters. The song was a spoof of Fiddlers' Dram's 'Day Trip to Bangor', a national top three hit at the start of the year. It had come about because Mike Smith, the Capital Radio breakfast-show presenter (and, like Roger, a future Radio 1 DJ), often had to read out cancellation notices for the 8.14 a.m. train from Barnhurst to Blackfriars on his morning travel update. It thus became a standing joke that the service never actually ran.

Roger's afternoon drive-time shows became immensely popular with Londoners, generating such features as the 'Three O'Clock Thrill' and the jingle 'Grab a Little Piece of Heaven', which was specially recorded for him by David Dundas. In 1976, his regular Friday rush-hour oldies show, *Cruisin'*, acquired a cult following largely due to him playing obscure rockabilly records to the London audience, who were hearing many of them for the first time. As a real music fan, however, Roger not only revered the oldies but always sought out the best new releases across all genres. He was noted for his broad tastes and for championing Dolly Parton and The Stranglers, among others.

With his love of The Beach Boys' music, Roger also helped to spread the word about the Knebworth Rock Festival in June 1980. The line-up for the event that year included Mike Oldfield, Santana, Lindisfarne, and The Blues Band, and the headlining Beach Boys had just released a new album, *Keepin' the Summer Alive*. In anticipation of the festival and a series of two concerts by the group shortly afterwards at the Wembley Empire Pool (later the Wembley Arena), Roger asked listeners to vote on their all-time fifteen top Beach Boys hits of all time. Two subsequent Fridays were used to play back the top songs coupled with interviews with all the group members. After the Wembley concerts had been played and recorded to soundboard, he broadcast one of them in his Friday-night live-concert series. History had been made, though nobody recognised it at the time, as these would be the last gigs featuring the group's original line-up before the death of drummer Dennis Wilson in December 1983. Roger's interview with Dennis was the last the latter ever completed; other stars interviewed for Capital by Roger included David Bowie, Kate Bush, Lionel Richie, Mick Jagger, and each member of Queen.

In 1984, Roger presented a radio documentary series, *Sergeant Pepper's Lonely Hearts Club Band: A History of The Beatles Years*, for Westwood One in America. Featuring nine programmes just under an hour in length, and researched by Beatles expert Mark Lewisohn, it used archive interview material and music from Abbey Road Studios to present an in-depth portrait of the group's career. He was also regularly in demand to conduct interviews with American artists, and Westwood One would fly him over to their studios for the purpose.

For some of his colleagues, Roger was the DJ's DJ. David Jensen once said that he elevated the art of being a presenter far above the usual banter, saying that 'his succinct style and dry wit never interfered with the flow of music, for which he had a genuine love and enthusiasm'. While Paul Gambaccini was a student at America's Dartmouth College in the 1970s, he had regularly listened to Roger's shows; he later stated that Roger was his main inspiration in becoming a DJ himself.

None of Roger's contemporaries revered him more than Bob Harris. Having left Radio 1 for a while and *The Old Grey Whistle Test* on BBC2 television, Bob was working on Radio 210 Thames Valley while Roger was at the helm on the Capital Radio afternoon show. Roger, he readily admitted, was 'something special'. He was modest and bright, with a great voice, a dry sense of humour, and a wicked laugh—to say nothing of his gift of making the listener feel as if he was speaking directly to him or her. He never lost sight of the fact that the primary function of a good DJ is to highlight the music. The records he played included quality rock and pop, rock 'n' roll, soul, 60s oldies, album tracks and rarities, and no rubbish. He enhanced it with his casual knowledge, clearly borne of a deep love of what he chose. To Bob, Roger's style was 'a rarefied mix that proved to [him] that it was possible to do a mainstream radio programme packed full of high-quality music and still make it really accessible'.[7] Moreover, Bob continued, Roger had perfect microphone technique. He stood apart from most other DJs in that he never used blocking devices or surged the music up and down while he was speaking. Once a record had started playing, he never touched the faders or chased the fades. He had an innate sense of word economy, setting his voice level just above the volume of the music, blending in with it perfectly. All in all, it was 'a masterclass in microphone technique'. He was informative, he loved his music, and time and time again he presented the ultimate musical package.[8]

Bilingual Canadian radio personality Marc Denis, who had long been a regular listener to Roger on 1470 CFOX, always credited him with being the main inspiration for him 'getting into [the] crazy radio business'. In September 1983, Marc was sent to cover the temporary opening of the Abbey Road Studios to the public for French radio and TV in Quebec. Roger invited him to the Capital studios, where they chatted for about an hour before his programme began. Even better was to come for Denis; he and his producer, Gerry Dixon, went down during a break to the Thames for Greater London Day and were delighted to witness live music from Mungo Jerry, The Troggs, and The Swinging Blue Jeans. Marc had been introduced to those groups by Roger in the mid-1960s, when the latter had been on the radio in Montreal.

Roger was his own man; he believed that rules were there to be broken. On one show, he gave an exclusive airing to a new track by Paul McCartney. It was not merely the latest single or a track off a recent album, not even a radio session, but a brand-new song recorded the previous day at Abbey Road Studios. As it had not been cleared for airplay, the publishing, Performing Right Society, and other legal formalities had not been completed. Hearing it coming out of the speakers, a furious Tim Blackmore, with the sound of writs ringing in his ears, stormed into the on-air studio to remonstrate with his errant presenter and ask how he had obtained it. Scott stared at him innocently before explaining that he had just played a tape in a plain brown envelope that suddenly appeared on his desk, and he had no idea where it came from.

Phil Swern, his producer, had known Roger ever since he joined Capital Radio, even though at first it was only on 'grunting terms in the corridor'. When the station launched a Sunday lunchtime music quiz show, *You Ain't Heard Nothing Yet*, with Capital DJs versus pop stars and other guests, he was in charge of compiling the questions. At first, Roger was a notable absentee from the host team. When Phil asked, 'Why no Roger?', back came the unanimous response that he would surely never take part. 'Shall I ask him?' he suggested. Aware that Roger had acquired a reputation for being distant and not always approachable, he knocked on the office door one day, introduced himself, and asked him if he would like to participate.

'I was wondering how long it would take you to ask me!' was the instant reply.

When Capital announced that it was going to launch its gold service and run it every Sunday as an experiment, Roger was an obvious choice as the first presenter, and Phil was given the job of building the programmes. He was slightly in awe of Roger, and with some trepidation he put a running order together and came up with a final list of sixty records. Having completed the task, it then took him four days to pluck up the courage to present Roger with a script, his hands trembling. 'You understand it's only a rough running order,' he explained apologetically, 'it'll all change before the show goes out.'

Roger spent what seemed an eternity absorbing the list, apparently tut-tutting and generally looking dissatisfied, with Phil increasingly convinced that he hated every record on there. When he had finished, he looked at Phil and asked, 'Well—why would you want to change anything?'

For fifteen mostly very happy years, Capital Radio was Roger's home. However, as the 1980s drew to a close, the standardised, computerised playlists, market and audience research, and other techniques introduced by the commercial stations were no longer for him. He wanted to play as much Bruce Springsteen, Bob Seger, Paul McCartney, or Beach Boys as he pleased, no matter what the controller thought was best for listeners (or the station's advertisers).

Where commercial radio went wrong, he believed, was in its obsession with the bottom line and profits. It was indeed a business, and they were in it to attract audiences and make money—not just for their presenters to spread the word about the music that they loved—but as in all things, a compromise between the two could surely be reached. However, what Roger termed as 'horrifying things' were done in the name of research; auditorium testing and research could be carried too far, and Roger argued that they were. It was all very well for stations to come up with their own Top 20 chart, but when playlists were drawn up by a computer, 'with no input from the guy on the air', it was evident that all the excitement, the heart and soul, had been wrenched from it. Where was the possibility of making mistakes, the element of risk and danger that kept everyone on their seats, the excitement of discovering something new and sharing it? All that was gone in the name of playing safe. Some faceless power had come up with a list of records that would prevent listeners from switching off. 'Don't play anything dangerous that might rock the boat,' Roger scathingly summed up the new approach, 'or people might turn off.' Had such a principle been applied in the mid-1950s, the Light Programme might have stuck unendingly to a diet of Mantovani and Bing Crosby, ignoring rock 'n' roll altogether.

Towards the end of his life, Roger delivered a hard-hitting verdict on the sad state of the prevailing policy in broadcasting, particularly where commercial radio was concerned:

> If I was going into radio now—I wouldn't, because the whole excitement of it was to find something new, and you want to put it on this gigantic record player you've got, and play it for all those other people and see what they think of it—isn't it great? That was more than half the joy of it, having this record you've just found, and wanting to share it with all these other people, not going in there with a sheet of paper which has gone through a computer, has been researched and there's your list of records, and get on there and do it. There's no excitement in that, so as a result everything you hear is manufactured. It's all artificial excitement. And I believe that people—I can hear it made up—I can hear those people sitting there thinking 'I don't really want to be doing this, but it's better than working for a living.'[9]

Although only a minor Top 100 hit in Britain, one record he eagerly championed and with which he would always be associated was a track by

Marc Germino. The American songwriter's second album, *Caught In The Act Of Being Ourselves*, contained a song named 'Rex Bob Lowenstein', a wry, country-style ballad about a veteran breakfast DJ, 'forty-seven going on sixteen', on the mythical radio station WANT. Bob has eclectic tastes and an adoring audience who appreciate his acceptance of their requests, mixing them in with whatever he feels like playing at any given time. One line in the song goes: 'He'll play Stanley Jordan, The [Grateful] Dead and Little Feat, and he'll even play the band from the college down the street'. All is well until the day when a suited businessman who knows and cares nothing about music takes the station owner out to lunch and tells him how he can increase his ratings by adhering to 'a songlist'. When Rex is informed that in future he will play only what he is told to, he locks himself in the studio and goes mad on air, still playing exactly what he wants. He his eventually dragged into court for reasons the judge apparently fails to understand, but His Worship wryly closes his summing-up by thanking the prisoner 'for playing "Moon River" last night'.

Like many other DJs across the world, Roger readily identified with this classic song. He might have been forgiven for thinking that it was about him; he played it regularly, and from then on he and his memory would invariably be associated with it. Luckily, Roger enjoyed the freedom that many real-life Rex Bob Lowensteins evidently never did.

Nevertheless, that freedom would be curtailed all too suddenly with changes in top management at Capital; Roger soon sensed that these changes were not for the better. The spectre of the songlist was looming large, and he feared that his musical instincts would be curbed. BBC Radio, he admitted, was the last refuge of the free spirit. While the Corporation had its own rigid controls, it was nowhere near as restricting as the regime that he could foresee soon being introduced in the commercial sector. Total anarchy did not work, he conceded, but there had to be room for manoeuvre. When Johnny Beerling made him an offer to join Radio 1 and work with a sympathetic producer, promising plenty of control over what would be in the programmes, he could hardly say no. Phil Swern was the obvious choice as producer, and when Roger Scott asked him to join him, his reaction was, 'You don't need me.'

'You're the only person I trust,' Roger insisted.

Before Roger could take the step from commercial radio to the station that he had once derided as a 'dinosaur', he received even worse news. Despite only being in his early forties, he was diagnosed with stomach cancer. His wife, Lesley, told friends that the prognosis was good as the disease had been caught in the early stages, and he was admitted to hospital in Slough. However, the surgery was mismanaged; after being discharged, he was taken seriously ill again and admitted to another hospital, this time in Harefield, where he nearly died. Nevertheless, he made a partial recovery and his cancer officially entered remission.

At around the same time, June 1988, he was back on Radio 1 after fifteen years with Capital. In his eyes, the Corporation was no longer the Civil Service-like institution it had seemed to be at the start of his career in Britain, when he had used the alias of 'Bob Baker'. For the first time since his brief stint some fifteen years earlier, he was broadcasting to a national audience. With him came producer Phil Swern, who was by now noted as having one of the largest private record collections of all time.

Provision was made for Roger to present two regular shows at weekends. The first was *Saturday Sequence*, an afternoon show that he took over from Johnnie Walker. It featured mainly album tracks alongside interviews with artists including Jackson Browne, Dion, John Cougar Mellencamp, and Don Henley, as well as an 'in concert' slot. Johnnie had just left Radio 1 for the second time, lured away by Richard Branson to join his new satellite station, 'Radio Radio', which never really got off the ground and made him wish he had stayed put. His loss, in the short term at least, was Roger Scott's gain. Roger, whom Johnnie acknowledged was 'one of the best music and on-air jocks we've ever had', was thrilled to step into the vacancy. Every time he got home from a show, he was grinning from ear to ear, telling Lesley that it was his idea of 'radio heaven'. Why Johnnie Walker would ever want to leave such a show was beyond him.[10]

The second was *Scott on Sunday*, which went out late at night from 11.00 p.m. to 2.00 a.m. This programme was more eclectic, with a discerning choice of contemporary music (as in the previous day's programme) integrated with a helping of 1950s rock 'n' roll, soul, and a few classic pop and rock oldies from the 1960s onwards, with an eye for some of the less obvious choices. For example, The Supremes' 'Back in my Arms Again' was just as worthy of airplay, he said, as 'Where Did Our Love Go', even if it had not been as successful and was less well-remembered.

As ever, Roger's dry sense of humour was undimmed. Opening one *Scott on Sunday* in July 1989, at around the time of the 200th anniversary of the French Revolution, he remarked that he had just been reading an article about it in one of the colour supplements and had discovered that the trouble started because somebody had had a late lunch. Another week, he confided his thoughts on barbecues, asking what was it about people in Britain who had the urge to sit outside eating burnt food whenever the sun came out. Despite his dislike of appearing on television, if he had lived longer, Roger—like so many of the other Radio 1 names before him—might have been persuaded to grasp the nettle and front *Top of the Pops*.

The cancer hung like the Sword of Damocles over what should have been the most glorious phase of a career that had the potential to run and run. When Tim Blackmore asked him if he was frightened, Roger shook his head. 'I'm not frightened any more—just curious.' Roger's fine sense of irony was demonstrated when he played the Hollies' 'I'm Alive' to open his first Sunday evening show after going public with the news. By this time he was relying largely on hope, painkillers, alternative remedies, and sheer willpower, but nothing could disguise his rapid downhill descent.

Roger had known writer and broadcaster Lesley-Ann Jones ever since he took her under his wing as an assistant while she was a post-university intern at Capital. She later stated that while his health was deteriorating, he found solace in the music of The Neville Brothers. Keith Richards had played guitar on their album *Uptown* in 1987, and he introduced Roger to the group in person. Their follow-up album, *Yellow Moon*, was released in 1989. The album contained two songs in particular—'Healing Chant' and a cover of Bob Dylan's 'With God on our Side'—that 'turned Roger inwards and most lifted his soul' during his final months.[11]

The disease had returned with a vengeance, and Roger battled until he was too ill to carry on. His last words to his listeners came at the end of what was to be his final show, at 2.00 a.m. on 9 October 1989. After his closing record, the Beach Boys' 'Heroes and Villains', were, 'Thank you for your company, thank you for your support and thank you for your kindness. I hope I'll see you next weekend but there are no guarantees.' They were brave words; sadly, there was indeed no guarantee, let alone another programme.

Two weeks later, he asked friends and colleagues to join him in a celebration of his forty-sixth birthday at Wembley Park restaurant. Invitations went out with the instruction that the party would go ahead regardless of whether or not he was still there to share it with them. He was there by the skin of his teeth, in a wheelchair, but by 9.00 p.m. he was exhausted and ready to go home. Just before he left, Alan Freeman helped the guests to raise the roof with 'For He's a Jolly Good Fellow'. It was clearly in the nature of a farewell.

One week after that, on the night of 30 October, he rang Tim Blackmore to say that he felt he had reached the end, that he wanted to thank him for being a good friend, and goodbye. He had not expected to survive the night. The next morning, as he woke up, his first words to his wife Lesley were, 'Oh my God, am I still here?' A few hours later, he was gone.

The overnight three-hour show was taken over briefly by Andy Peebles before Bob Harris, who had returned to Radio 1 only a few months earlier, took over on a regular basis. Pleased as he was to be back, he admitted that it was in the saddest of circumstances. Taking over from Roger Scott was a case of 'huge boots to fill'.[13]

Alan Freeman, Chris Tarrant, and Tim Blackmore all spoke at his funeral at Slough Crematorium on 8 November, attended by 250 fans as well as various people from the music industry. That same week, Alan, who always recognised in Roger the same pride and passion that had also motivated him to become a DJ, presented a tribute in the occasional Radio 1 documentary series *Radio Radio*. It was a ninety-minute show based largely around Roger's recollections, which he had recorded not long before his death.

Also broadcast on the station a few weeks later was the recording of a celebration held at Abbey Road Studios on 7 December, attended by music friends, fellow DJs, and around 250 fans. It was hosted by Alan Freeman, who dedicated the show to the memory of the man whose 'commitment to good music dominated everything'. Dave Edmunds and Nick Lowe, who had been regular studio guests of Roger during his Capital days, played Everly Brothers songs live for listeners in what was their first performance together for eight years, singing 'Poor Jenny' and 'Here Comes the Weekend'. Cliff Richard contributed 'Move It', Chris Rea 'I Left my Heart in San Francisco' and Mark Knopfler the very appropriate 'Feel Like Going Home'. Tributes were read out from admirers such as the Bee Gees, U2, and Tom Petty, who called him 'one of those rare, refreshing people who was in the music business solely because he loved music'. The climax of the occasion was a recorded message from Roger in which he talked about his basic love of music and his longing to share it with listeners. It was followed by a solo performance of 'Rex Bob Lowenstein' from Mark Germino, who had flown in from America for the occasion.

Lesley-Ann Jones was one of those who treasured Roger's memory, remarking that his generosity of spirit and knowledge of music was unsurpassed. He had been a very dear friend, and thanks to him she had had the opportunity of meeting the likes of Bruce Springsteen, Elton John, Billy Joel, David Bowie, and Fleetwood Mac with him on trips to Miami, Los Angeles, New York, and Montreux. In the process, he had taught her more about music than anybody else she had ever known.

Roger's elder son by his first marriage, Graham, followed in his father's footsteps. Imbued with the same passion for music, he went to Canada and became a presenter on CFOX 99.3 FM in Vancouver and Sonic 102.9 in Edmonton. Tragically, his career was also cut short; he passed away in 2011 at the age of thirty-eight. As in the case of his father, a real broadcasting talent had been taken far too soon.

Endnotes

Introduction

1. *The Times*, 20 October 2009.
2. Ward, p. 116.
3. Walker, p. 196.
4. Peel, *Margrave*, p. 402.
5. Garner, p. 21.

Chapter 1

1. Leigh, pp. 167–8.
2. BBC News online obituary, 2 September 2013.
3. Jacobs, *Jacobs' Ladder*, pp. 84–5.
4. *Ibid*. p. 91.
5. *The Independent*, 3 September 2013.
6. *The Daily Mail*, 3 September 2013.
7. *Ibid*.
8. Leigh, p. 188.
9. Jacobs, *Jacobs' Ladder*, pp. 148–9.
10. *Ibid*. p. 174.
11. *Ibid*. p. 171.
12. Kynaston, p. 373.
13. *The Independent*, 3 September 2013.
14. BBC News online obituary, 2 September 2013.
15. Richards, p. 166.
16. *Radio Rewind* interview, undated.
17. Jacobs, *Jacobs' Ladder*, p. 138.
18. *Radio Rewind* interview, undated.
19. *Ibid*.
20. *News of the World*, 29 January 1967.
21. *The Times*, 29 May 1967.

22. *Ibid.* 25 May 1968.
23. *Basingstoke Gazette*, 13 July 2011.
24. *Radio Rewind* interview, undated.
25. *David Jacobs, On The Record*, Radio 2, 2 and 9 March 2011.
26. *Radio Times*, 3 October 1998.
27. Random Radio Jottings, David Jacobs, http://andywalmsley.blogspot.co.uk/2013/12/radio-lives-david-jacobs.html
28. *The Daily Telegraph*, 4 September 2013.
29. Random Radio Jottings, David Jacobs.
30. Harris, p. 260.
31. *Radio Times*, 3 October 1998.
32. *The Times*, 19 and 20 September 2007.
33. *David Jacobs, On the Record*, Radio 2, 2 and 9 March 2011.
34. *Ibid.*
35. *The Guardian*, 3 November 2007.
36. *Radio Times*, 3 October 1998.
37. Alex Lester talking to Jeremy Vine, Radio 2, 3 September 2013.
38. Jacobs, *The David Jacobs Collection*, Radio 2, 4 August 2013.
39. *The Daily Telegraph*, 7 August 2013.
40. *The Jewish Chronicle*, 25 July 2013.

Chapter 2

1. *Radio Times*, 'My Kind of Day', 14 January 1989.
2. *The Complete Fluff*, Radio 2, 29 December 2001.
3. *Radio Rewind* interview, undated.
4. Bowden-Smith, K., 'All Systems Freeman', www.transdiffusion.org/2006/12/31/all_systems_fre
5. *The Complete Fluff*, Radio 2, 29 December 2001.
6. *Ibid.*
7. Gillan, p. 50.
8. *Radio Times*, 1 October 1977.
9. *Nova Lepidoptera*, 1, May 1988.
10. Interview, *The Complete Fluff*, Radio 2, 29 December 2001.
11. *Alan Freeman's Classical Bits*, booklet notes, BBC, 1999.
12. *Radio Times*, 1 October 1977.
13. *The Complete Fluff*, Radio 2, 29 December 2001.
14. *Daily Express*, talking to Judith Simons, 1978.
15. *Nova Lepidoptera*, 1, May 1988.
16. *Ibid.*
17. *Ibid.*

18. *Radio Times*, 'My Kind of Day', 14 January 1989.
19. *Kaleidoscope*, Radio 4, 16 August 1997.
20. *The Times*, 29 November 2006.
21. *Mail on Sunday*, 'You', 30 June 1991.
22. *Ibid.*
23. *The Times*, 28 December 1992.
24. Garfield, p. 43.
25. *Ibid.* p. 31.
26. *The Daily Telegraph*, 2 December 2006.
27. *This Is Your Life*, ITV, recorded 14 December 1995, shown 24 January 1996.
28. *The Complete Fluff*, Radio 2, 29 December 2001.
29. *The Independent*, 29 November 2006.
30. *The Daily Telegraph*, 2 December 2006.
31. BBC News online, 28 December 2006.

Chapter 3

1. Garfield, p. 259.
2. BBC, 'Keeping it Peel', http://www.bbc.co.uk/radio1/johnpeel/biography/1930s/1939-1959/
3. Heatley, p. 20.
4. Peel, *Margrave*, p. 85.
5. Heatley, p. 40.
6. Peel, *Margrave*, p. 173.
7. *Ibid.* p. 177.
8. Garfield, p. 257.
9. *The Guardian*, 1 August 2001.
10. Peel, *Margrave*, p. 232.
11. *Ibid.* p. 170.
12. *Radio Times*, 30 April 1982.
13. *Let It Rock*, January 1973.
14. *Keep On Rockin'*, Autumn 1996.
15. Peel, *Margrave*, p. 271.
16. *Ibid.* p. 275.
17. *Ibid.* p. 225.
18. *Ibid.* pp. 239–40.
19. Garner, p. 82.
20. *The Listener*, 7 June 1973; Peel, *Olivetti*, pp. 311–2.
21. Peel, *Margrave*, p. 302.
22. *Ibid.* p. 300.

23. Garfield, p. 268.
24. Heatley, p. 33.
25. Peel, *Margrave*, pp. 80–1.
26. Sounds, 20 July 1974; Peel, *Olivetti*, p. 352.
27. Garner, p. 92.
28. *Ibid.* p. 89–90.
29. Heatley, p. 105.
30. Peel, *Olivetti*, p. 183; *Listener*, 22 December 1977.
31. Jones, pp. 81–2.
32. Peel, *Margrave*, p. 259.
33. Heatley, p. 116.
34. Peel, *Margrave*, p. 313.
35. *Ibid.* p. 312.
36. *Ibid.* p. 311.
37. Interview with David Hepworth, *Smash Hits*, 4 October 1979.
38. Margrave, p. 348.
39. *The Listener*, 10 July 1988; Peel, *Olivetti*, p. 158.
40. Peel, *Margrave*, p. 240.
41. *The Guardian*, 10 August 2014.
42. Walker, p. 187.
43. Harris, pp. 64–5.
44. Andy Kershaw interview with Nick Duerden, *The Independent*, 29 September 2010.
45. Peel, *Margrave*, p. 377.
46. *Observer*, 9 March 1986; Peel, *Olivetti*, p. 153.
47. *Observer*, 23 August 1987; Peel, *Olivetti*, p. 155.
48. Heatley, p. 135.
49. Garfield, p. 265.
50. Garner, p. 12.
51. Garfield, p. 270.
52. *The Independent*, 6 January 1987.
53. *Radio Times*, 12 May 2001; Peel, *Olivetti*, p. 18.
54. BBC News online, 26 October 2004.
55. Peel, *Margrave*, p. 180.
56. *The Independent*, 25 August 1989.
57. Peel, *Margrave*, p. 358.
58. *The Guardian*, 26 October 1994; Peel, *Olivetti*, p. 8.
59. Peel, *Margrave*, p. 181.
60. Garfield, pp. 257–8.
61. Radcliffe, p. 159.
62. Peel, *Margrave*, pp. 349–52.
63. Heatley, p. 23.

64. *Radio Times*, 29 August 1997, 5 September 1997.
65. Heatley, p. 165.
66. *Radio Times*, 17 October 2014.
67. Heatley, pp. 166–7.
68. Radcliffe, pp. 99–100.
69. Peel, *Margrave*, p. 378.
70. Garfield, p. 262.
71. Peel, *Margrave*, p. 1.
72. Heatley, pp. 166.
73. *Ibid.* p. 148.
74. Garfield, p. 259.
75. Heatley, p. 171.
76. Radcliffe, p. 159.
77. Peel, *Margrave*, p. 253.
78. BBC News online, 27 October 2004.

Chapter 4

1. *Sounds*, 28 March 1981.
2. Clark, p. 113.
3. *Ibid.* p. 145; Offshore Echos, http://www.offshoreechos.com/Tommy%20Vance.htm
4. *Observer*, 4 December 2005.
5. Radio London obituary, http://www.radiolondon.co.uk/jocks/tommy/tommyobit.html
6. Offshore Echos.
7. Public Image Ltd Archive, Capital Radio interview with Johnny Rotten, http://www.fodderstompf.com/ARCHIVES/REVIEWS%202/capital77.html
8. *Sounds*, 28 March 1981.
9. Garner, p. 104.
10. *Sounds*, 28 March 1981.
11. *Radio Rewind*, interview, undated.
12. *Sounds*, 28 March 1981.
13. *Ibid.*
14. *Ibid.*
15. *Ibid.*
16. *Ibid.*
17. *Radio Rewind*, interview, undated.
18. 'Joe Elliott remembers Tommy Vance', Teamrock, http://www.teamrock.com/features/2015-03-96/joe-elliott-remembers-tommy-vance

19. *Offshore Echos*,
20. *Ibid*.
21. *Radio Rewind*, 'Tommy Vance: Remembered', http://www.radiorewind.co.uk/radio1/tommy_vance_tributes_page.htm
22. *Observer*, 3 December 2005.

Chapter 5

1. *Radio Radio*, Radio 1, 8 November 1989.
2. *Ibid*.
3. *The Daily Telegraph*, 2 November 1989.
4. *Radio Radio*, Radio 1, 8 November 1989.
5. *Ibid*.
6. *The Daily Telegraph*, 2 November 1989.
7. Harris, pp. 115–6.
8. *Ibid*. pp. 116–7.
9. *Radio Radio*, Radio 1, 8 November 1989.
10. Walker, p. 304.
11. Lesley-Ann Jones, 31 October 2014, http://lajwriter.blogspot.co.uk/2014/10/grab-little-piece-of-heaven-with-roger.html
12. Harris, p. 257.

Bibliography

Books

Blackburn, T., *Poptastic! My Life in Radio* (Cassell, 2007); *The Living Legend: An Autobiography* (W. H. Allen, 1985)

Cavanagh, D., *Good Night and Good Riddance: How Thirty-Five Years of John Peel Helped to Shape Modern Life* (Faber, 2015)

Clark, R., *Radio Caroline and the True Story of the Boat that Rocked* (History Press, 2014)

Garfield, S., *The Nation's Favourite: The True Adventures of Radio 1* (Faber, 1998, revised 1999)

Garner, K., *The Peel Sessions: A Story of Teenage Dreams and One Man's Love of New Music* (BBC, 2007)

Gillan, I., *Ian Gillan* (Blake, 1998)

Grace, A., *The Link With Home—Sixty Years of Forces Radio* (Services Sound & Vision Corporation, 2003)

Harris, B., *Still Whispering After All These Years: My Autobiography* (Michael O'Mara, 2015)

Heatley, M., *John Peel: A Life in Music* (Michael O'Mara, 2004)

Jacobs, D., *Jacobs' Ladder* (Peter Davies, 1963); (with Freeman, S.) *Caroline* (Hutchinson, 1978)

Jones, D., *Elvis Has Left the Building: The Day the King Died* (Duckworth Overlook, 2014)

Kershaw, A., *No Off Switch: The Autobiography* (Serpents' Tail, 2011)

Kynaston, D., *Modernity Britain: A Shake of the Dice, 1959–62* (Bloomsbury, 2014)

Leigh, S., *Frank Sinatra: An Extraordinary Life* (McNidder & Grace, 2015)

Peel, J., and Ravenscroft, S., *Margrave of the Marshes* (Bantam, 2005)

Peel, J., *The Olivetti Chronicles: Three Decades of Life and Music* (Bantam, 2008)

Radcliffe, M., *Thank You For The Days: A Boy's Own Adventures in Radio and Beyond* (Simon & Schuster, 2009)

Richards, K., *Life* (Little, Brown, 2010)

Rider, D. (comp.), *Happy Birthday Radio 1: Ten Years 1967–77* (Everest, 1977)
Street, S., *The A to Z of British Radio* (Scarecrow, 2009)
Walker, J., *The Autobiography* (Michael Joseph, 2007)
Wall, M., *John Peel—A Tribute to the Much-Loved DJ and Broadcaster* (Orion, 2004)

Internet Sources

All accessed between July and November 2015.

980 CKGM Montreal Super 70s Tribute Pages (http://www.marcdenis.com/ckgm.asp)
BBC, 'Keeping it Peel' (http://www.bbc.co.uk/radio1/johnpeel/biography/1930s/1939-1959/)
Bowden-Smith, K., 'All Systems Freeman' (http://www.transdiffusion.org/2007/02/01/all_systems_fre)
Denis, M., 1470 CFOX Montreal Radio Archive (http://www.marcdenis.com/cfox/)
Jones, L., blog (http://lajwriter.blogspot.co.uk)
Offshore Echos, (http://www.offshoreechos.com/Tommy%20Vance.htm)
Public Image Ltd Archive, Capital Radio interview with Johnny Rotten, 16 July 1977 (http://www.fodderstompf.com/ARCHIVES/REVIEWS%202/capital77.html)
Radio London, 'Tommy Vance Obituary' (http://www.radiolondon.co.uk/jocks/tommy/tommyobit.html)
Random Radio Jottings (http://andywalmsley.blogspot.co.uk/2013/12/radio-lives-david-jacobs.html)
Teamrock (http://www.teamrock.com/features/2015-03-96/joe-elliott-remembers-tommy-vance)

Journals, Newspapers, and Fanzines

Daily Mail
Keep On Rockin'
Let It Rock
Observer
Radio Times
Smash Hits
The Daily Telegraph
The Guardian
The Independent
The Times

Index

101ers, The 71
10cc 71
5000 Volts 119
AC/DC 46, 72, 98, 103, 106, 109

Adams, Bryan 103
Adrian, Jon ('Softly') 107-8
Adverts, The 73
Ahern, Mike 63
Altered Images 74
Althea and Donna 174
Amen Corner 65
Andrews, Bernie 63, 64, 67
Argent 43
Asher, Jane 19
Aspel, Michael 25, 27, 29, 55, 82
Attlee, Earl Clement 15

Bad Company and Rodgers, Paul 33, 103
Baker, Danny 73
Bance, Greg 114
Bannister, Matthew 54, 84, 106
Barlow, Gary 57
Barron Knights, The 107
Bates, Simon 54, 58, 59, 101-102, 105, 108
Batt, Mike 71
Bay City Rollers, The 70, 120
Bebop Deluxe 71
Beach Boys, The 121, 124, 127; Wilson, Dennis 144

Beatles, The 13, 20, 41, 46, 62, 72, 80, 91, 97, 98, 103, 112-113, 115-117, 121; Harrison, George 20, 78, 113; Lennon, John 20, 59, 65, 71, 117; McCartney, Paul 20, 41, 58, 123-124; Starr, Ringo 20
Bee Gees, The 59, 128
Beefheart, Captain, and his Magic Band 62, 95
Beerling, Johnny 45, 50, 57-58, 65, 84, 102, 125
Belle and Sebastian 77
Bennett, Tony 81
Berlin, Irving 125
Berry, Chuck 13
Berthoud, Chris 83
Birch, Philip 93
Birkin, Jane, and Gainsbourg, Serge 50
Bizet, Georges 46
Black Sabbath 45, 105
Black, Don 30
Blackburn, Tony 30-31, 38-39, 55-56, 63, 71, 75-76, 102
Blackmore, Tim 45, 48-50, 56-57, 59, 123, 127-128
Blair, Tony 33, 85
Blues Band, The 121
Blur 77
Bogarde, Dirk 44
Bolan, Marc and T. Rex/Tyrannosaurus Rex 59, 64, 67

Bonzo Dog Doo Dah Band, The 88
Boomtown Rats, The 73
Boston 97
Bowie, David 74, 95, 121, 128
Boyd, Alan 31
Boys of the Lough, The 73
Bradlaw, Patricia 24
Brambles, Jakki 83
Branson, Richard 82, 103, 126
Brewer, Teresa 45
Brooke, R. H. J., ('Brookie') 60, 64
Brown, Craig 55, 58
Browne, Jackson 126
Browne, Tom 45
Bruce, Ken 29-30
Buckley, Tim 95
Buffalo Springfield 46
Bukht, Michael 118
Bush, George W. 85
Bush, Kate 121
Buzzcocks, The 72

Caballe, Montserrat 46
Campbell, Glen 92
Campbell, Nicky 59, 81, 84
Cara, Irene 79
Caravan 45, 65
Carpenters, The 68, 118
Carrington, Desmond 28, 31
Cash, Dave 94, 99, 108, 118
Chambers, Dwain 107
Chapman, Mike, and Chinn, Nicky 120
Charles, Prince of Wales 85, 103
Chinnery, Derek 16, 37, 45, 48, 53-54, 72, 75, 84, 97
Clapton, Eric 71-72; Derek and the Dominoes, 99
Clark, Petula 22, 117
Clarke, John Cooper 74
Clarke, Stanley 97
Clash, the 72, 74, 101

Clooney, Rosemary 16, 34
Cochran, Eddie 68
Cocker, Jarvis 79, 88
Cocker, Joe 69
Cogan, Alma 15
Cohen, Leonard 64
Cole, Gracie 16
Collins, Joan 49
Constanzo, Jack 92
Cooder, Ry 71
Cook, Peter 44
Coral, Bernie and Diana 51
Corbett, Ronnie 29
Covay, Don 71, 80
Crawford, Michael 27
Cream 71
Critchley, Julian 23, 25
Crosby, Bing 16, 25, 31, 124
Cushing, Peter 44

Dalglish, Kenny 86
Damned, The 72
Damone, Vic 15, 25, 29
Dane, Rick 63
Dave Clark Five, The 112
Davies, Gary 54
Dawn 68
Day, Aidan 48
Dean, Larry 113
Dee, Simon 22, 56
Deep Purple 41, 45-46, 99, 103–105, 108; Gillan, Ian (including the group Gillan) 40, 58, 103, 108-109; Glover, Roger 41; Lord, Jon 41, 108
Def Leppard and Elliott, Joe 104
Dell, Alan 16, 23
Denis, Marc 122
Denny, Sandy 71
Diamond, Neil 75
Diana, Princess of Wales 85
Dinosaur Jr 105

Dion (Dion DiMucci) 126
Dion, Celine 56
Dire Straits 103; Knopfler, Mark 128
Dixie Dregs, The 96
Dixon, Gerry 122
Domino, Fats 68
Donegan, Lonnie 88
Donovan, Jason 52
Douglas, Lesley 29
Drummond, Pete 63
Dundas, David 121
Dunn, Clive 43
Dupree, Simon, and the Big Sound 42
Dvorak, Antonin 46
Dylan, Bob 45, 68-69, 72, 127

Eagles, The 73; Henley, Don 126
Easton, Sheena 78, 80
Eddie and the Hot Rods 71
Edmonds, Noel 23, 29, 49, 58
Edmunds, Dave 72, 74, 128
Electro Hippies, The 81
Elizabeth II 16
Ellis, James 90
Emerson, Lake and Palmer 45-46, 51, 68, 97
Enfield, Harry 55
Engelmann, Franklin 16
Episode Six 40
Epstein, Brian 13, 62
Evans, Chris 29-30
Evans, Ken 15
Everett, Kenny 65, 89. 94-95
Everly Brothers, The 110, 128

Fahey, Brian 37
Fairport Convention 88
Faith No More 105
Faith, Adam 13
Fall, The 74, 80, 83, 86, 88, 105; Smith, Mark E. 74
Fame, Georgie 23

Farnon, Robert 26
Farren, Mick 64
Fatback Band, The 71
Fayed, Dodi 85
Fiddlers' Dram 121
Fitzgerald, Ella 15, 28
Fleetwood Mac 73, 128
Fordyce, Keith 36-37
Four Brothers, The 83
Fox, Neil 56
Frankie Goes To Hollywood 49
Franklin, Aretha 47, 79, 81
Free and Rodgers, Paul 33
Freeman, Alan 25, 76, 97, 108, 119, 127-128; early life and career in Australia, and singing lessons 33-35; settles in England 35-36; with Radio Luxembourg 36-37; with BBC Light Programme and Radio 1 37-42, 45, 50; Pick of the Pops 38-39, 41-42; catchphrases and origin of 'Fluff' nickname 38; Top of the Pops 21-22, 40; Juke Box Jury 40, 49; All Systems Freeman 41; album sleeve notes 42; film roles and commercials 44; Saturday Rock Show 45-7; rock and classical jingles 46; leaves Radio 1 for Capital 48-9; appoints Tim Blackmore manager 49; depression 50; on Classic FM; ill-health 56; Their Greatest Bits, retirement, and death 57-59
Freeman, Sue 21

Gabor, Zsa Zsa 18
Gambaccini, Paul 56, 58-59, 88, 108, 122
Game, The 22
Garden, Graeme 70
Gardner, Ava 15
Garland, Judy 15
Gee, Buddy 116

Geesin, Ron 64
Genesis 45, 97
George VI, King 83
Germino, Marc 125, 128
Gershwin, George 25
Gilbey, Ryan 86-87
Gillett, Charlie 45
Ginsberg, Allen 117
Glitter, Gary 68, 95
Golden Earring 104
Goulet, Robert 31
Grateful Dead, The 64, 72, 125
Greedies, The 73
Greer, Charlie 115
Grisewood, Freddie 23
Grundy, Bill 72, 95-96

Hagopian, Dean 115
Haley, Bill, and his Comets 13
Hall, Tony 31
Hammill, Peter 95
Handel, Georg Frideric 46, 83
Hanson, Susan 93
Harper, Roy 74
Harris, Bob 27, 31, 54, 76, 122, 127
Harvey, PJ 77
Hatch, David 26
Hatch, Tony 30
Hearne, Bill 92
Hendrix, Jimi 46, 62, 64, 72, 93
Herman, Jerry 27
Herman's Hermits 42, 92, 112
Hill, Benny 14
Hird, Thora 19
Hitchcock, Alfred 19
Holland, Jools 23
Holly, Buddy 110
Hope-Weston, Jessie and Stella 108
Horne, Nicky 48, 69, 119
Howerd, Frankie 29
Humperdinck, Engelbert 42

Hurll, Michael 79

Ifield, Frank 13
Incredible String Band, The 62
Instone, Anna 30, 39
Iron Maiden 104
Ivy League, The 57

Jack The Lad 71
Jackie (Challenor) and the Commuters 121
Jackson, Jack 36-37
Jacobs, Caroline 24
Jacobs, David 37, 38, 40, 44, 51; early life and career 13-14; with BBC Light Programme and Radio 2 14-16, 23, 25-6, 28-31; with Radio Luxembourg 15; with BBC television and ITV 16-17, 27; Juke Box Jury 17-21, 22-23; Top of the Pops 21-22; as author 21; Any Questions? 23-24; family life 24-25; independent radio 25-26; compilation albums 28; last show and death 31
Jacobs, Jeremy 24
Jacobs, Lindsay, née Stuart-Hutcheson 24, 30, 32
Jam, The 73
James, Elmore 88
Jefferson Airplane 62, 64
Jensen, David ('Kid') 53, 55, 75, 79, 96, 103, 122
Jethro Tull 46, 97
Joel, Billy 128
John, Elton 46, 68, 128
Johnson, Duncan 108
Johnson, Linton Kwesi 99
Jones, Lesley-Ann 127-128
Jones, Paul 22
Jones, Quincy 45
Judas Priest 104, 109
Juste, Adrian 108

Index

Keating, Ronan 57
Keen, Alan 61-62
Keith, Alan 29, 56
Kennedy, John F. 61
Kennedy, Nigel 46
Kensit, Patsy 44
Kern, Jerome 25
Kershaw, Andy 76, 87
King Crimson 45
Kitt, Eartha 19
Kutner, Jon 96

Laurel, Stan, and Hardy, Oliver 71
Lawley, Sue 83
Leary, Timothy 117
Led Zeppelin 44, 47, 72, 97- 99, 117; Page, Jimmy 44; Plant, Robert 70, 117
Ledger, Cat 86
Lee, Peggy 34
Lester, Alex 30-31
Lindisfarne 66, 121
Lindsay, Robert 108
Lone Star 72
Long, Janice 75, 79
Love Sculpture 41
Lowe, Nick 72, 128
Lynn, Vera 16-17, 29-30
Lynyrd Skynyrd 99

MacInnes, Colin 44
Madonna 78
Mahavishnu Orchestra 97
Manfred Mann 22
Manic Street Preachers 105
Margaret, Princess 83
Marine Offences Bill 93
Marley, Bob and the Wailers 71
Marmalade, The 66
Marriott, Bryant 41
Marsh, Richard and Caroline 24
Martin, Sir George 13, 97, 109

Martino, Al 16
Martyn, John 73
Maschwitz, Eric 18
Matthew, Brian 28, 36, 37
Mayall, John & The Bluesbreakers 97
McCullough, Dave 98, 100
McLaren, Malcolm 95
McRae, Carmen 19
Meat Loaf 46, 103
Medicine Head 70, 73
Mellencamp, John Cougar 126
Metcalfe, Jean 37, 61
Michael, George 79
Michelmore, Cliff 61
Milburn, Shirley Anne 61, 70
Milligan, Spike 19
Minogue, Kylie 52
Misty in Roots 83, 88
Misunderstood, The 61, 80
Mitchell, Guy 34
Mitchell, Joni 71
Mitchell, Leslie 17
Moffat, Roger 23
Molesters, The 97
Monks, The 49
Monro, Matt 15, 22, 28
Moore, Ray 25
Moss, Don 23, 38
Mothers of Invention, The 22
Motors, The 73
Mott/Mott The Hoople 69, 119
Move, The 42, 64, 80; Wayne, Carl 93
Mungo Jerry 122
Murray, Pete 18, 21
Murray, Ruby 15
Musicians' Union 16, 36, 66
Myer, Jon 39, 109
Myners, Neil 57

Napalm Death 81
Neville Brothers, The 127

New Order 88
Nice, The 97
Nile 81
Nilsson 80
Nirvana 105
Noakes, Rab 74

O'Rahilly, Ronan 92
Ocean, Billy 103
Oddie, Bill 69-70
Oldfield, Mike 68, 121
Ono, Yoko 65, 117
Orbison, Roy 19, 81, 83
Orbital 88
Osmonds, The 66
Oswald, Lee Harvey 61
Outsiders, The 73

Pablo, Augustus 95
Paige, Elaine 49
Parker-Bowles, Camilla 85
Parker, Graham and The Rumour 72-73
Parkinson, Michael 25
Parton, Dolly 121
Peebles, Andy 127
Peel, John, 41, 55, 93, 94, 96-99, 102, 105-106, 108, 112, 119-120; birth and early life 60-61; in USA 61; first marriage 61, 70; with Radio London 62; The Perfumed Garden 62, 93; as journalist 62, 66, 85; joins Radio 1 62-3; Top Gear 63-64; compilation albums 64; Night Ride 64; Top of the Pops 65, 78-9, 82; Dandelion label 69-70, 80; second marriage 70; Festive 50 72, 73; punk rock and change of programme's musical policy 71-74; other Radio 1 DJs 75-77; at Peel Acres 77; family life 77-78; football and Hillsborough tragedy 77, 81; shyness 81-82; other TV and Radio 4 work 82-83; awarded OBE 85; political opinions 85-86; ill-health 86; begins memoirs 86-87; death and tributes 87-89
Pellow, Marti 56
Perry, André 117
Pertwee, Jon 16
Peters, Lee 93
Petty, Tom 128
Pink Floyd 45, 62, 64, 72, 99, 109, 114
Porter, Cole 25
Powell, Enoch 24
Powell, Peter 74
Presley, Elvis 13, 22, 60, 66, 68, 73, 110
Pretty Things, The 46
Price, Alan, Set 63, 80
Principal Edwards Magic Theatre 69

Queen 46, 71, 79, 120-121

Rachmaninov, Sergei 83
Racing Cars 74
Radcliffe, Mark 84-85, 87
Radha Krishna Temple 117
Rainbow 46, 98, 103
Ramones, The 71
Ramsay, Gordon 107
Ravenscroft family 77; Alan 61; Florence ('Flossie') 60; Sheila (née Gilhooly) 67, 70, 76-78, 81, 86-87
Rea, Chris 128
Read, Mike 82
Reed, Jimmy 83
Reeves, Martha and the Vandellas 42
Reynolds, Gillian 31
Rezillos, The 74
Rice, Sir Tim 30, 119
Richard, Cliff, and the Shadows 13, 110, 128
Richard, Little 13, 21, 79
Richie, Lionel 121

Richman, Jonathan and the Modern Lovers 71
Riley, Marc ('Lard') 85
Roberts, Harry, Sound 40
Rolling Stones, The 13, 20, 28, 47, 62, 91, 98, 112; Jagger, Mick 20, 92, 103, 121; Jones, Brian, 20; Richards (formerly Richard), Keith 20, 92, 127
Rose, Billy 13
Rose, Tim 64
Roseman, Jon 107
Rosko, 'Emperor' 106
Ross, Jonathan 73
Runyon, Damon 85

Saints, The 72
Sam (Moore) and Dave (Prater) 80
Samson 97
Santana 97, 121
Sargent, Sir Malcolm 13
Savile, Jimmy 21-22, 37, 40, 50, 65, 70
Saxon 104
Scorpions, The 109
Scott, Graham 128
Scott, Lesley 125-127
Scott, Robin 63
Scott, Roger, early life and career 110-112; in USA and Canada 112-117; with John Lennon and Yoko Ono 117; on Radio 1 118, 125-7; on Capital Radio 118-123; on television 119; disenchantment with commercial radio 123-124; illness, death, and tribute 125-128
Seger, Bob 124
Sellers, Peter 17
Selwood, Clive 63, 69
Sex Pistols, The 47, 72-74, 78, 95; Jones, Steve 78; Rotten, Johnny (John Lydon) 49, 72, 95
Sham 69 74; Pursey, Jimmy 73
Shanghai 72

Shapiro, Helen 19
Shenton, Joan 95
Sinatra, Frank 15, 22, 25-26, 28, 31, 34-35
Siouxsie and the Banshees 73, 80
Skinner, Richard 106, 108
Slade 68, 95
Slits, The 97
Smith, Mike 121
Smothers, Tommy 117
Soft Machine 64
Solomon, Phil 94
Spain, Nancy 19
Spector, Phil 92
Spencer Davis Group, The 42
Springsteen, Bruce 69, 120, 124, 128
St John, Bridget 64, 69
Stackwaddy 69
Stapleton, Cyril 16
Starr, Kay 34
Status Quo 29, 45, 73-74, 80, 86
Stewart, Johnnie 17, 19, 21
Stewart, Rod 66, 68, 71; Faces, The 66-67
Stiff Little Fingers 74
Stoehr, Robert 118
Stone, Christopher 35, 36
Stranglers, The 47, 72, 121
Strawbs, The 65
Sturgess, Claire 54, 105
Sunny Ade and His African Beats 71
Supremes, The 126
Sweet, The 67-68, 71
Swern, Phil 50-51, 57, 123, 125-126
Swinging Blue Jeans, The 112, 122
Sykes, Eric 19

Tabor, June 73
Talmy Stone Band, The 40
Tarrant, Chris 47, 128
Taylor, Derek 117
Tchaikovsky, Pyotr Ilyich 46
Teal, Clare 30, 31
Ten Years After 65

Thatcher, Margaret 24
Thin Lizzy 73
Thom, Jim 91
Thomas, John Charles 33
Todd, Ann 38
Tomorrow 64
Traffic 64
Traveling Wilburys, The 81
Travis, Dave Lee 29, 44, 54-55, 59, 75, 79
Tremeloes, The 91
Troggs, The 122

U2 128
Undertones, The 74, 80, 83, 88; Sharkey, Feargal 88
Uriah Heep 97

Van der Graaf Generator 73, 97
Vance, Tommy 54-55, 63-64, 112; early life and career 90-91; professional name 91; in USA 91-92; as recording artist 92; on Radio Caroline 92; on Radio London 93; on Radio 1 94, 96-100, 102-106; TV work 94, 106-107; voiceovers for commercials 94, 101; on Capital Radio 94-96; on Radio Victory and BFBS 95; Friday Rock Show 96-97, 99-100, 103, 105-106; Top of the Pops 101; commercial recording studios 103-104; Monsters of Rock compere 103; on GLR 104; on Virgin Radio, Classic Rock, and VH1 106, 108; death and funeral 108-9

Vibrators, The 97
Village People, The 101
Vow Wow 97

Wagner, Richard 46
Walker Brothers, The 120
Walker, Johnnie 30, 56, 69, 71, 76, 89, 126
Wall, Mick 93
Walters, John 60, 63, 67-68, 72-73, 74, 77, 80-81, 84-85, 87, 97
Ward, Clifford T. 70
Wells, John 65
Weston, Diana 108
Whiley, Jo 54
Whitcomb, Ian 92
White Stripes, The 80
White, Mark 62
Whitehouse, Paul 55
Whitesnake 103
Whitfield, June 30
Whitford, Gary 26
Whitney, John 120
Who, The, and Daltrey, Roger, 101
Wilson, Harold 65
Wilson, Tony 45, 50
Winter, Edgar, Group 46
Winton, Dale 58
Wogan, Terry 30, 63, 76, 119
Woolmans, Mike 104
Wright, Steve 84

Yes 45-46, 65, 68, 97
Young, Jimmy 37, 63
Young, Neil 109